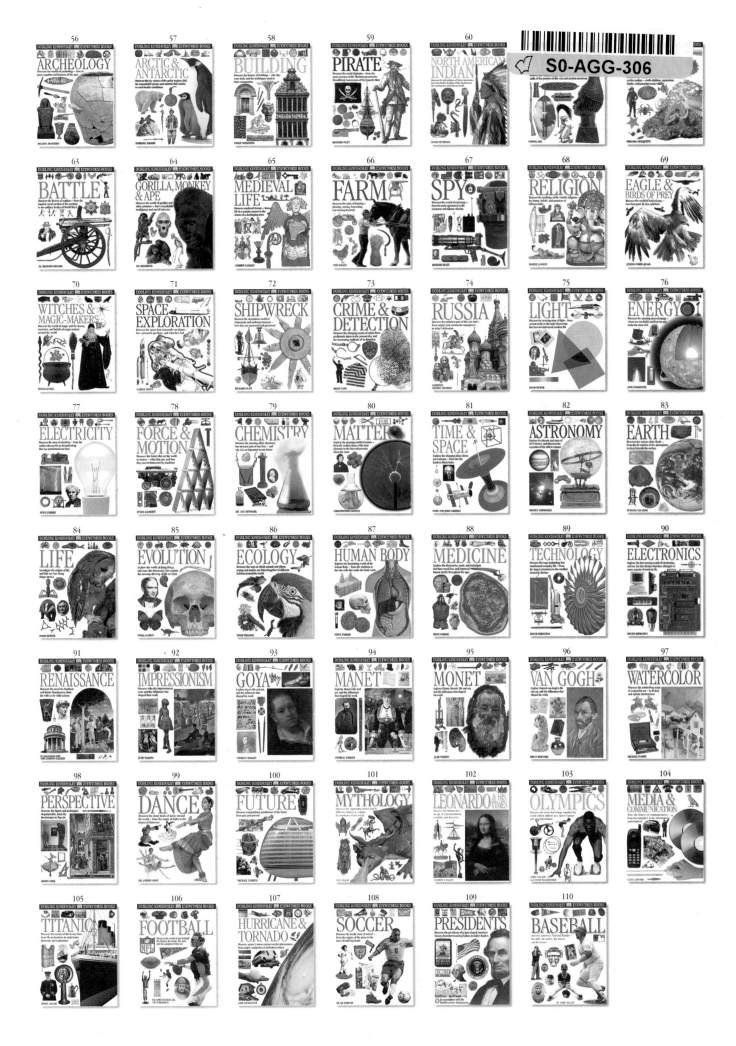

VAN GOGH

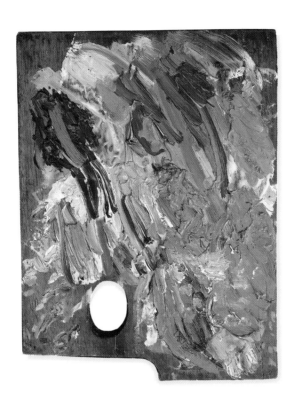

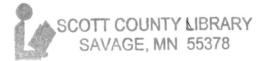

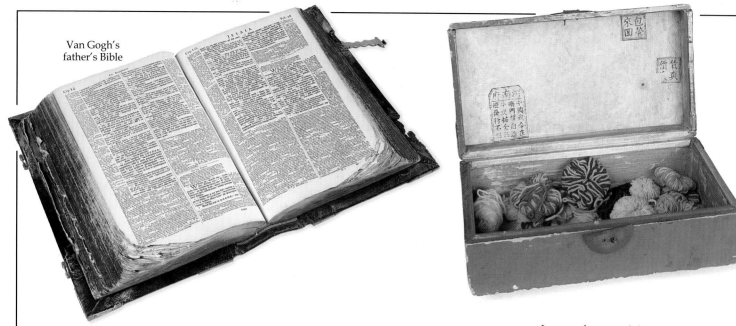

Van Gogh's
father's Bible

Japanese box containing
colored wools

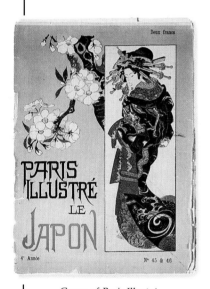

Cover of *Paris Illustré*,
copied by van Gogh

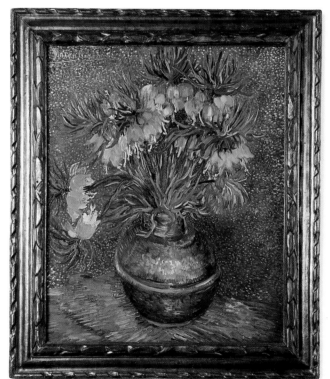

Fritillarias, 1887

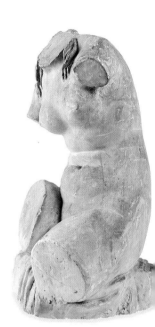

Plaster cast, owned
by van Gogh

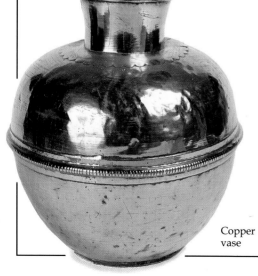

Copper
vase

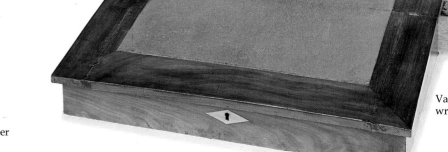

Van Gogh's
writing desk

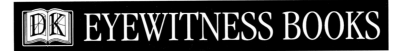

EYEWITNESS BOOKS

VAN GOGH

BRUCE BERNARD

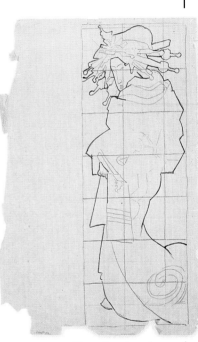

Trace drawing of
cover of *Paris Illustré*

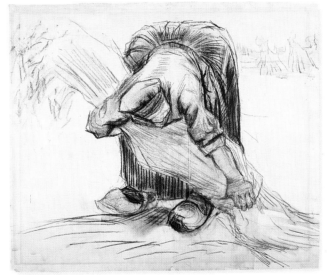

Charcoal drawing of Woman Binding Sheaves of Corn, 1885

Charcoal

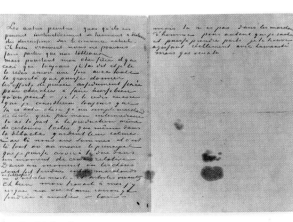

Van Gogh's last letter,
found on his body

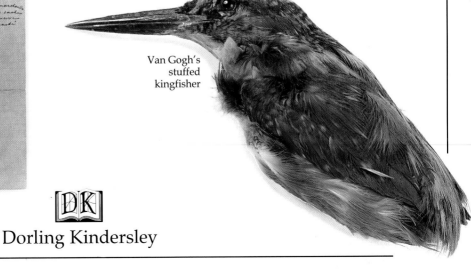

Van Gogh's
stuffed
kingfisher

DK

Dorling Kindersley

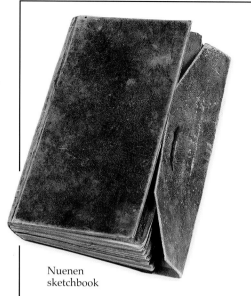

Nuenen
sketchbook

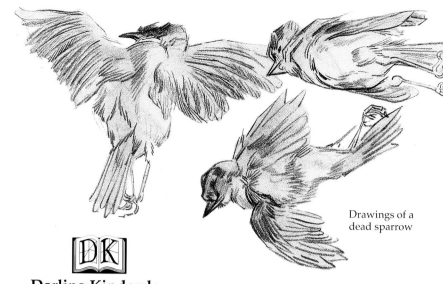

Drawings of a
dead sparrow

DK

Dorling Kindersley

LONDON, NEW YORK, AUCKLAND, DELHI, JOHANNESBURG, MUNICH,
PARIS and SYDNEY

For a full catalog, visit

DK www.dk.com

Editor Phil Hunt
Assistant editor Luisa Caruso
Art editor Mark Johnson Davies
Design assistant Claire Pegrum
Series editor Gwen Edmonds
Series art editor Toni Rann
Managing editor Sean Moore
Editorial consultant Patricia Wright
Managing art editor Tina Vaughan
DTP manager Joanna Figg-Latham
DTP designer Doug Miller
Production controller Meryl Silbert
US editor Laaren Brown

This Eyewitness ® Book has been conceived by
Dorling Kindersley Limited and Editions Gallimard

© 1992 Dorling Kindersley Limited
Text copyright © 1992 Bruce Bernard
Introduction © 1992
This edition © 2000 Dorling Kindersley Limited
First American edition, 1999

Published in the United States by
Dorling Kindersley Publishing, Inc.
95 Madison Avenue
New York, NY 10016
2 4 6 8 10 9 7 5 3 1

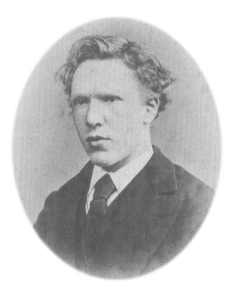

Vincent van Gogh

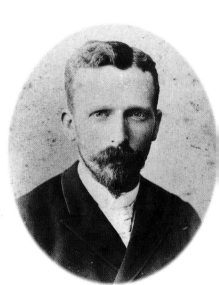

Theo van Gogh

Dorling Kindersley books are available at special discounts for bulk purchases for
sales promotions or premiums. Special editions, including personalized covers,
excerpts of existing guides, and corporate imprints can be created in large
quantities for specific needs. For more information, contact Special Markets Dept.,
Dorling Kindersley Publishing, Inc., 95 Madison Ave., New York,
NY 10016; Fax: (800) 600-9098

Library of Congress Cataloging-in-Publication Data
Bernard, Bruce.
Van Gogh / written by Bruce Bernard.
p. cm. — (Eyewitness Books) Includes index.
1. Gogh, Vincent van, 1853-1890—Criticism and interpretation.
I. Title II. Series.
ND653, G7B35   2000
759.9492—dc20   92–7061
                                                    CIP
ISBN 0-7894-6190-0 (pb)   ISBN 0-7894-4878-5 (hc)

Color reproduction by Colourscan, Singapore
Printed in China by Toppan Printing Co. (Shenzhen) Ltd.

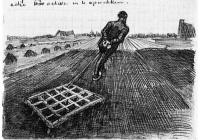

Letter
to Theo
van Gogh

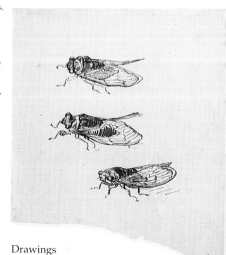

Drawings
of cicadas

Contents

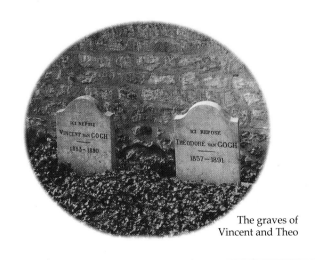

The graves of
Vincent and Theo

Youth and family

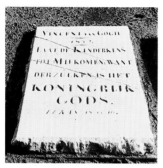

BROTHER'S GRAVESTONE
Vincent was born exactly one year after his stillborn brother, also named Vincent. Their names and the coincidence of their birthdays must have affected the artist's image of himself.

H ERE BEGINS the story of one of the greatest and most remarkable European painters of the 19th century. Vincent van Gogh was born on March 30, 1853, in the village of Groot Zundert, in the North Brabant region of the Netherlands. He spent the first 16 years of his life there before moving to The Hague, where he worked for his uncle as a clerk for the art dealers Goupil and Co. His roots lay firmly with his family, and the love he felt for his parents was reciprocated. It was not long, however, before Vincent's obstinacy and his struggle with religion would put a strain on the family, especially his father and his brother, Theo.

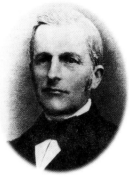

Theodorus van Gogh

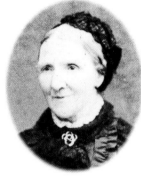

Anna Carbentus

VINCENT'S PARENTS
Theodorus van Gogh (b. 1822) was married to Anna Cornelia Carbentus (b. 1819). Theodorus was known as "the handsome parson," and, though an amiable man, was undistinguished as a preacher. Anna Carbentus, the daughter of a bookseller, was kind and respected, but sometimes alienated by the difficult character of her eldest son. Vincent would dearly have liked their complete approval and understanding, but he would go on to cause considerable anguish for two exemplary parents of their class and time.

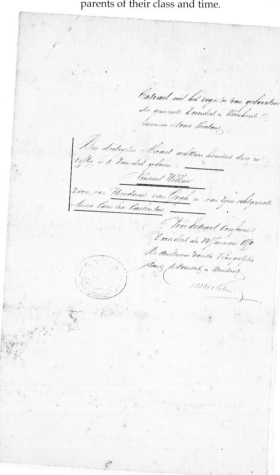

THE EARLY YEARS
As his birth certificate (above) shows, Vincent was born in Groot Zundert, where he attended the village school. He then studied under the family governess, moving on to a private, then a secondary school. He unaccountably left at the age of 15, and spent a year at home before deciding to enter the art trade – a natural move as three of his uncles were art dealers.

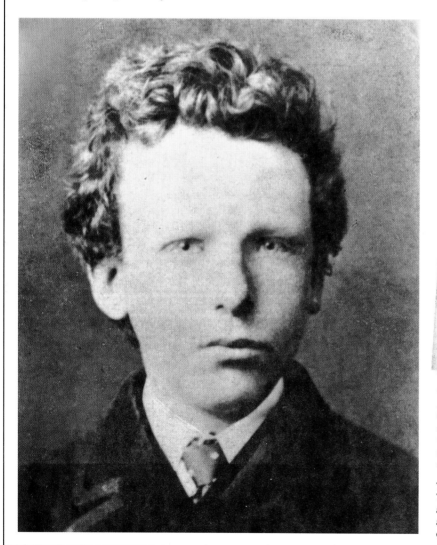

THE ARTIST AS A YOUNG MAN
This is one of only two photographs of van Gogh's face – here aged 13. His sister Elizabeth described him as looking old for his age, but said that "he was remarkable at such an early age because of the profoundness that was expressed in his whole being...."

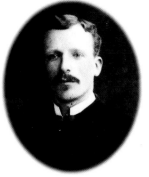

Anna

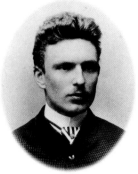

Theo

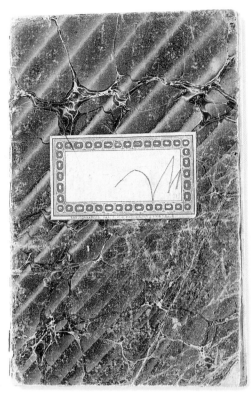

Cornelius (Cor)

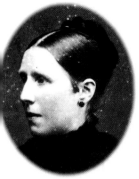

Elizabeth (Lies)

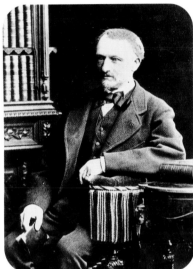

Wilhelmien (Wil)

BROTHERS AND SISTERS

Vincent's sister Anna was two years younger, and they were initially good friends when both were working in England. Theo was two years younger than Anna. Elizabeth (Lies) was two years younger again, and though not close to Vincent, published her memories of him in 1910. Wilhelmien (Wil) was nine years younger than her eldest brother and corresponded with him from his Paris days. Cornelius (Cor), 13 years Vincent's junior, would, like his brothers, die a tragic death, committing suicide in 1900.

UNCLE CENT

Vincent's Uncle Cent was a successful art dealer whose full name was also Vincent van Gogh. In 1858, the uncle was offered a partnership at Goupil and Co. in Paris, and he opened the branch in The Hague where Vincent went to work.

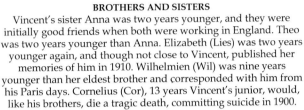

BETSY'S SKETCHBOOK

Vincent sent this sketchbook from London to Betsy Tersteeg, the daughter of the Goupil manager in The Hague. Hermanus Tersteeg thought highly of the young assistant, but he would later come to disapprove of van Gogh.

GOUPIL'S GALLERY

Van Gogh worked for nearly four years at his Uncle Cent's gallery in The Hague, to everyone's satisfaction. Here his almost inexhaustable appetite for looking at pictures and admiring their creators was born. "Admire as much as you can," he would soon write to Theo, but his enthusiasm invariably distorted his judgment; indeed, it always would to some extent. His whole family must have been pleased by his early success at Goupil's.

7

Life in England

IN MAY 1873, TWENTY-YEAR-OLD van Gogh arrived in England. He had been promoted to Goupil's London branch with a comfortable salary of £90 a year. He loved the city and, although initially disappointed in British art, soon came particularly to admire certain painters who expressed religious and moral sentiments. He became enthusiastic about English magazine illustrators and was also captivated by Charles Dickens and George Eliot. He fell in love with his landlady's daughter, Eugenie, who, unfortunately, was already engaged to be married (p. 10). Failure to win her hand may have caused the alienation that would lead to his dismissal from Goupil's, on his second posting to Paris. He returned to England in 1876 to teach first at Ramsgate and then Isleworth, where he also assisted his landlord the Rev. Slade-Jones in his church services at Turnham Green.

AN ADOLESCENT VINCENT
This photograph (above) shows van Gogh aged 19. He had red hair, blue-green eyes, and was heavily freckled. At 20 he went to London, buoyant from his success in The Hague, and, it is fairly certain, fell for Eugenie Loyer, his landlady's daughter. It has been thought that on declaring his love, he did not realize that she was already engaged, was shattered by the news, and left almost immediately. Recent disclosures suggest, though, that he knew of her engagement, perhaps tried to make her break it, and did not leave the house for some time. It was probably a key episode, but it remains an enigma.

RELIGIOUS CORRESPONDENCE
This letter to Theo (left) was written on school examination paper while Vincent was at Isleworth. It includes Longfellow's poem "I See the Lights of the Village" and ends with a heartfelt prayer, "May God unite us more and more and make us true brothers."

INFLUENCES
Longfellow's poem "Afternoon in February" was copied by van Gogh in his poetry album (left) and elsewhere. Opposite the copy (right) is an extract from "L'Amour," a poem by the French philosopher Michelet.

Longfellow's poem describes a funeral in winter and is a reflection of van Gogh's often melancholy state of mind

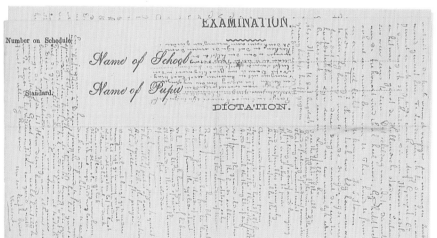

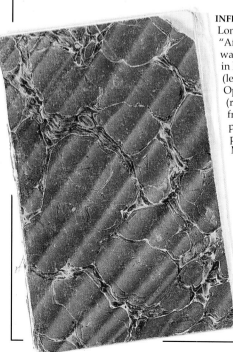

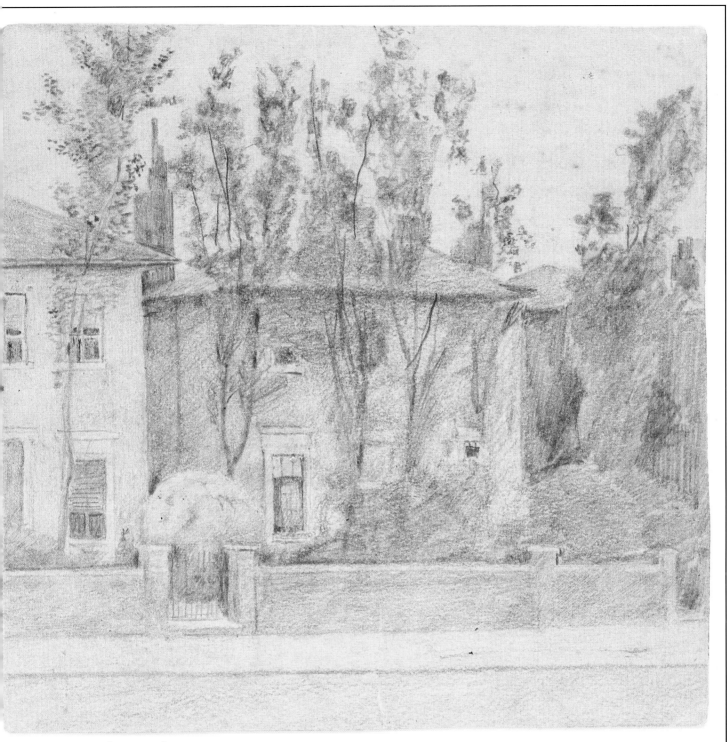

Houses at Isleworth

1876; 5¾ x 6 in (14.4 x 14.7 cm); pencil on paper

Van Gogh drew only infrequently until he started work in earnest in the Borinage (p. 10). The results vary considerably in quality, and while many are very acceptable efforts, they offer few glimpses of the great draftsman of the future. These houses, which may have been at Isleworth or Richmond, are executed in a somewhat tentative style, but may speak of the temporary peace of mind van Gogh found with the friendly clergyman who later visited him in Holland.

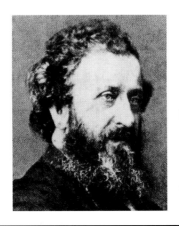

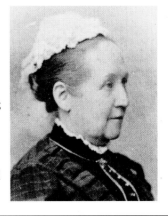

THE REV. AND MRS. SLADE-JONES
The Rev. Thomas Slade-Jones rescued van Gogh from his first unpaid post as a teacher, offering him £15 a year and his board.
The clergyman soon became aware of the young Dutchman's evangelical fervor and encouraged him. Slade-Jones and his wife, Annie, made a deep impression on van Gogh, and he meticulously copied many of his favorite texts into an album for her.

Preaching and poverty

VAN GOGH STILL HAD GREAT AFFECTION for England, despite his misfortune in love. Together with his ever-growing religious enthusiasm, his natural frugality enabled him to work as a schoolteacher. At the school in Ramsgate in 1876, he received no salary at all, and at Isleworth he was paid only £2 10s a month. Van Gogh was grateful to the Rev. Slade-Jones, but he returned to Holland in December 1876, working in a bookstore in Dordrecht before he failed in his studies for the ministry. In 1878, he moved to the Borinage, a Belgian coal-mining area, to work as a lay preacher. Although van Gogh was again seen as a failure, it was there he began to draw in earnest.

ECCE HOMO
This print of Christ crowned with thorns was inscribed in England for Theo at a time when van Gogh saw himself as his brother's spiritual mentor. The sentiment conveyed by an image was of paramount importance to van Gogh.

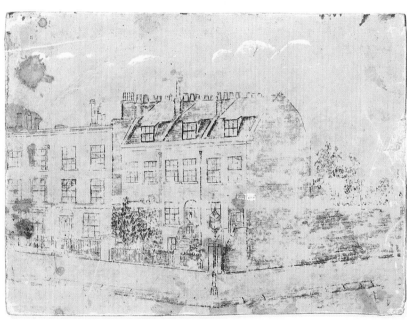

HACKFORD ROAD
This drawing by van Gogh of his lodgings at 58 Hackford Road, Brixton, was only discovered in 1972. The house is on the extreme left. Van Gogh moved into the home of Ursula Loyer in August 1873 and, according to letters from his sister Anna to Theo, fell in love with Ursula's daughter, Eugenie. He was certainly intensely happy there until a complex situation caused him great disappointment.

PETERSHAM LETTER
These drawings conclude a letter that contains a description of a walk between taking a Sunday school service at Turnham Green and preaching a sermon at Petersham. Both churches are sketched at the bottom of this letter, and the artist also wrote of having walked in darkness to London the morning before.

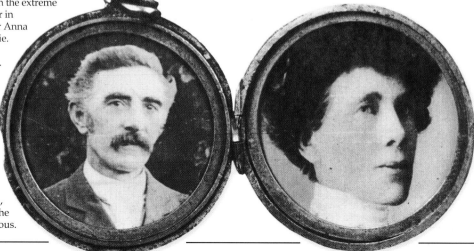

EUGENIE LOYER AND HER FIANCE
This locket contains photographs of Eugenie Loyer and Samuel Plowman, the man she married. Eugenie was engaged while van Gogh lived in the same house, and whatever passed between them started a chain of events that would bring his career in art dealing to an end, cause him eventually to leave England, and make him an ardent, though finally disenchanted, religious fanatic. Only then would he find the vocation that would make him universally famous.

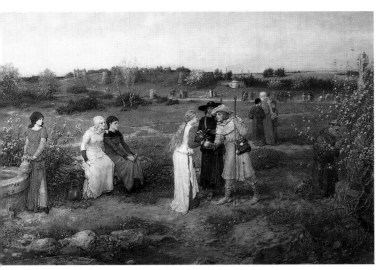

GOD SPEED!
George Henry Boughton; 1870; 48 x 72½ in (122 x 184 cm)
Van Gogh viewed this second-rate picture as a glorious vision of hard-won
redemption, showing how fanatical he was at the height of his religious enthusiasm.

PSALM BOOK
During his time in
the Borinage, van Gogh
worked in the coal-
mining communities of
Wasmes and Cuesmes.
He used a small psalm
book (right) as an aid to
preaching and annotated
many pages in his own
hand. Here it is shown
open at hymn 159, and
the highlighted verse
speaks of the consoling
powers of God – of
personal significance to
a man who was also
"sad and suffering."

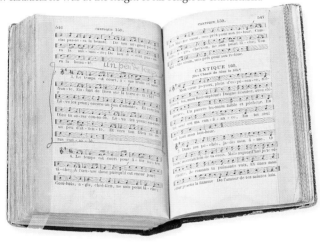

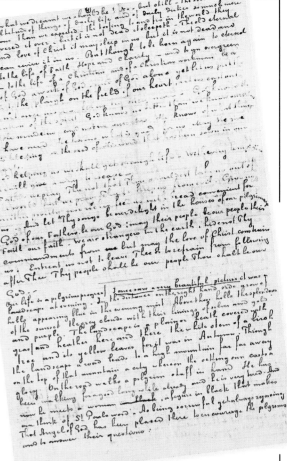

THE FIRST SERMON
In this extract from van Gogh's first sermon,
he imaginatively describes details of Boughton's
God speed!: "... the splendor of the sunset, the
gray clouds with their linings of silver and gold
and purple ... through the landscape is a road that
leads to a high mountain far, far away. On top of that
mountain is a city where the setting sun casts a glory."

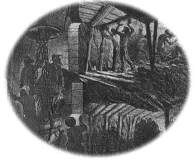

A GREAT SACRIFICE
Van Gogh gave all his surplus clothes to
the Borinage miners' families, but was
dismissed for his inadequacy as a preacher.

BEARERS OF THE BURDEN
This drawing represents the essential
character of van Gogh's evangelical
passion as it reached its peak in the
Borinage. The working women bear their
heavy burdens and their poverty but are
closer to Christ than the distant church is,
and their miners' lamps will show them
the way to salvation more surely than will
the ordinary light of day. Van Gogh shared
John Bunyan's conviction that the poor and
humble would find salvation more easily
than the rich, or than those attending the
essentially worldly Christian churches.

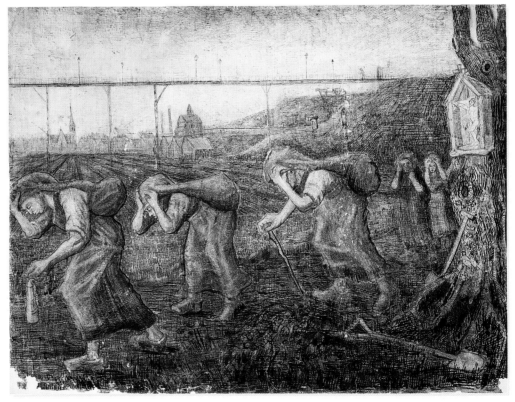

The image of the sower

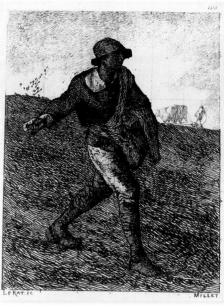

In 1881 van Gogh joined his parents in Etten; he grew up in the countryside and his most profound personal feelings would find their expression in subjects taken from the endless cycle of work in the fields. Many of the pictures that first excited van Gogh's interest in art were images of peasant life and labor. Jean-François Millet was the first painter to establish this kind of subject matter as a main theme, and van Gogh saw him as a great prophet. The first finished drawings he made at Etten, where his struggles as an artist began in earnest, were from engravings after Millet: *The Sower* was one of them. The sower and reaper are universal symbols, but no one before van Gogh invested either with such intensely personal feeling.

A RURAL SCENE
The ox-drawn plow was quite rare in northern Europe in the late 19th century. The horse that replaced it was, in its turn, superseded by the tractor.

LE RAT'S SOWER
Le Rat faithfully reproduced Millet's *Sower* in this etching. Van Gogh squared up the image and used it as the basis for his own *Sower* drawing (right). He viewed the sower as a figure of great significance and held Millet in high esteem. "I try to study that master seriously," wrote the artist with reverence.

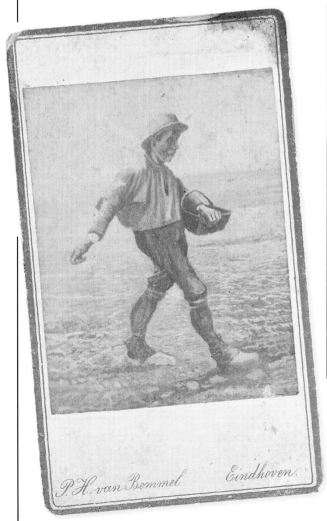

VISITING CARD
This *carte de visite* photograph (left), of a copy of *The Sower* (after Millet), was owned by van Gogh. The image had such emblematic force for him that he cared little about its quality. He may have acquired it in 1884 when he went to Eindhoven to help a retired goldsmith called Hermans decorate his room with farming scenes.

THE ANGELUS
Jean François Millet; 1877; 26 x 22 in (66 x 55.5 cm)
"Yes, that picture by Millet, *The Angelus*, that is it – that is beauty, that is poetry." Van Gogh's admiration for Millet was unbounded. The painting shows two peasants pausing for *The Angelus*, a series of prayers recited when the church bell was rung in the morning, at noon, and in the evening. While *The Sower* was seen as a radical statement about labor, the piety of *The Angelus* would be universally admired.

The Sower

881; 19 x 14½ in (48 x 36.5 cm); pencil, ink, and paint on paper

Millet's original composition was simple and masterly.
The forward motion of van Gogh's figure, more accentuated
by light in the original painting, is counterbalanced by the
outstretched right hand and trailing left leg. The oxen and
harrow preceding the sower draw the eye to the right,
but the direction they are going in leads it back through
the body to the hovering crows on the left.

THE PLOW
This plow is of
a design that was
in common use in the
late 19th century. It
demanded considerable
skill and strength to control
the plow's direction in
combination with the animal
that pulled it, whether it
was an ox or a horse.

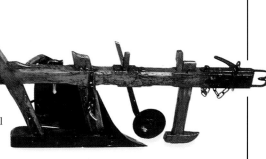

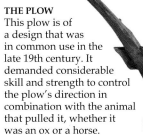

THE ROLE OF BIRDS
Van Gogh aimed
to produce his own
version of one of Millet's
masterpieces. However,
by copying from Le Rat,
he has altered the subject
matter: Millet painted
birds on the horizon of
The Sower, but van Gogh
has made them marks
of uncertain meaning.

**A BETTER
VERSION**
Van Gogh improved upon
Le Rat's undistinguished
etching. The crude
outlines of the latter's
work are reproduced, but
also made more sensitive.
The figure stands out
more effectively from
its background, which
itself seems more real.

HANDS AND FEET
The weakest part
of van Gogh's version
is perhaps the hands –
however, they are
equally ill-defined in
the etching. The feet
and legs are improved,
though – he made a
firmer pattern of the
folds in the breeches
and stockings.

RURAL THEMES
Of the three
fundamental images
of agriculture – sowing,
reaping, and plowing
– van Gogh made over 20
images of sowing, a few
less of reaping, and very
few of plowing. There
were also a number with
digging as their subject,
whether for cultivation,
the potato harvest, or
simply as studies of
figures in movement.

Etten and The Hague

V AN GOGH'S PROGRESS IN ETTEN was interrupted by an intense and unrequited love for his widowed cousin Kee Vos (née Stricker). On her decisive rejection of him he pursued her to Amsterdam, only to suffer further humiliation. Later in 1881, he moved to The Hague, where he took lessons from the painter Anton Mauve, a leading member of The Hague School, and a cousin of van Gogh's mother. This encouraged him to break with his father and settle there with Theo's support. He became involved with Sien Hoornik, a local woman and occasional prostitute, and set up house with her. He worked hard, but his character and unconventional way of life exasperated Mauve as well as van Gogh's father – who considered having him certified insane.

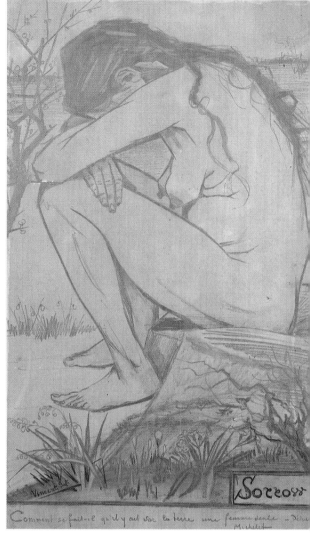

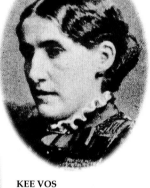

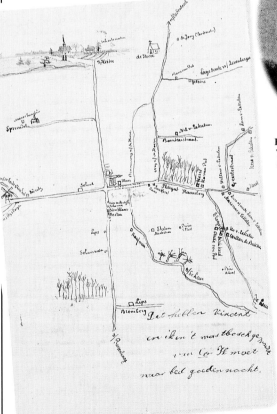

KEE VOS
The cousin with whom van Gogh fell so hopelessly in love was the widowed daughter of his mother's sister and Reverend Stricker. "No, at no time, never," were her words of rejection. Van Gogh found them difficult to accept.

SORROW
"I want to do drawings which touch some people," van Gogh wrote. " 'Sorrow' is a small beginning." His sympathy for women in distress was profound and self-defeating. This is the second of two versions, "touched up" from impressions he made of the first one through the paper. He embellished it for Theo with vegetation and the quotation from Michelet: "How can it be that there is on earth a woman alone, forsaken?" The woman was Sien, and her wretchedness is palpable.

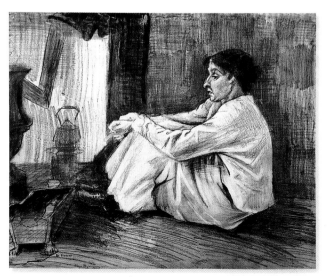

SIEN WITH CIGAR
Van Gogh's sympathy did not always spare Sien, and here, with her cigar, she is examined unblinkingly. She did, however, give van Gogh a sense of "great inner calm" that he never found in an intimate relationship again. Even though he might occasionally "fly into a rage" when drawing, he acknowledged that she was very patient with him. On finally breaking up with her, he wrote to Theo: "There is something between us which cannot be undone."

VAN GOGH'S MAP OF ETTEN
Etten, where van Gogh seriously began his career as an artist, was a fair-sized village with nearly 6,000 inhabitants, mostly Catholic. His father nonetheless had a large vicarage and medieval church. Van Gogh drew landscapes in the flat, often marshy countryside, and local people nearer home. He worked very hard, reputedly all night on some occasions. Conditions were almost ideal for the artist to develop his skills.

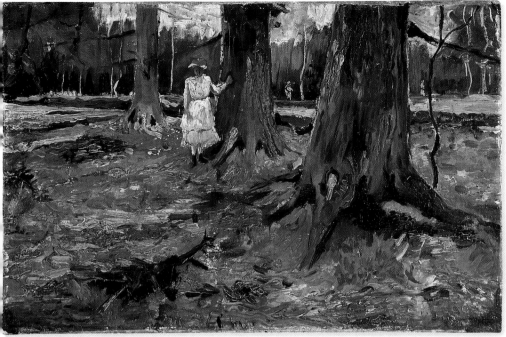

GIRL IN A WOOD
1882; 15 x 23¼ in (39 x 59 cm)
In The Hague, van Gogh was not in a hurry to paint in oils. At first he drew with a mixture of clumsiness and skill, and made many watercolor studies. But in August 1882, Theo visited him, and, impressed with his progress, provided money for paints. Then van Gogh set to work on seashore and forest scenes. This one appears to be an echo of England, and the season seems to have been advanced to convey a conventional sentiment of young girlhood among the autumn leaves. Only 25 oils survive from The Hague, but van Gogh told Theo he had left 70 behind on leaving for Drenthe (p. 16).

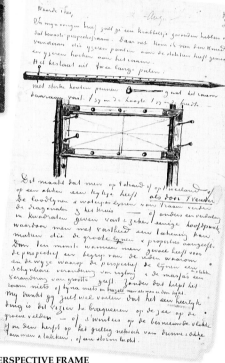

PERSPECTIVE FRAME
In 1882, van Gogh had a perspective frame (as sketched in the letter above) made to help him in both drawing and painting. This apparatus, in common use for centuries, remained of importance to van Gogh for some time, though in Arles he would proudly announce to Theo that he could work just as quickly without it.

VAN GOGH'S PRINTS
Prints in van Gogh's collection included Mr. Gradgrind (above) from Charles Dickens' *Hard Times* – the curious source for the figure (left). He also admired Luke Fildes' *The Empty Chair* (below).

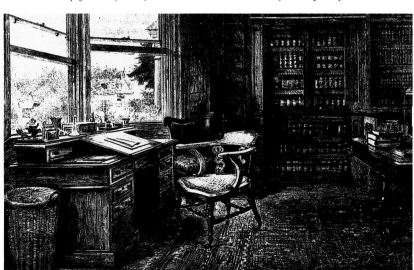

AT ETERNITY'S GATE
1882; 19¾ x 12¼ in (50 x 31 cm); lithograph on paper
This lithograph is from an incomplete series of eight in which van Gogh came closest to emulating his beloved British "Black and White" artists. He was delighted when a group of print workers asked for a copy of one of them to hang on their workshop wall. "I have tried to express the existence of God and eternity," he wrote. The pose could surely express grief or approaching death, but it was not intended to. The figure is as memorable and personal as that of "Sorrow" (left), and he would paint a version in entirely serene colors later at St. Rémy.

Peasants at work

When van Gogh left The Hague in September 1883, for the northern fenland of Drenthe, he did so with mixed feelings. He still felt guilty about leaving Sien and her child (p. 14), but he loved the landscape and worked as hard as the lack of studio, and a shortage of materials, would allow. He spent hours wandering the countryside, making sketches of the landscape, but began to feel isolated and concerned about the future. He wrote Theo 20 letters in 11 weeks – some rambling, others poetically descriptive. He had rented an attic in a house but found it melancholy, and was depressed with the quality of his equipment: "Everything is too miserable, too insufficient, too dilapidated." Physically and mentally unable to cope with these conditions any longer, he left for his parents' new home in Nuenen in December.

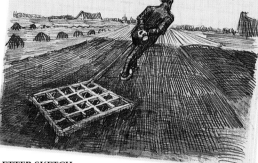

LETTER SKETCH
This drawing of a man pulling a harrow, with its dramatic recession to infinity, embodies van Gogh's vision of life as a road to fulfillment. His figure is a robust and confident one, and he may have been feeling so himself, if only for a moment or two, on his "pilgrim's progress." Vincent, writing to Theo about confidence, identifies himself with the peasant pulling the harrow through lack of a horse: "If one hasn't a horse, one is one's own horse."

THE HARROW
A harrow is an implement used to break up clods in the soil. In the 19th-century Dutch fenlands, it was often hand-pulled, as in the letter sketch (above).

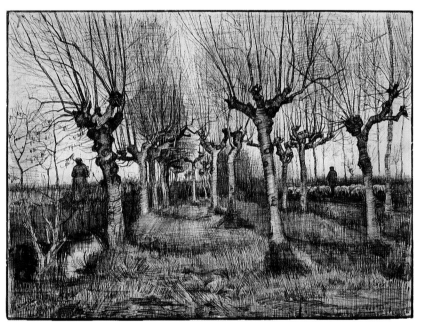

POLLARDED WILLOWS
In this drawing, and a few others made in the early spring of 1884, van Gogh showed how fluently he could wield a pen – using pencil as well, and no doubt employing the help of his perspective frame. He had hoped Theo might sell some ink drawings, but when Theo failed to do so, Vincent turned to black chalk. He did not return to the pen seriously until he reached Arles (p. 42); there, his natural brilliance in ink was demonstrated once again. Throughout van Gogh's career as an artist, and even at the beginning in Etten (p. 12), he showed signs of great virtuosity in drawing that he seems to have rejected or put aside. *Pollarded Willows* is an example of that talent shining through.

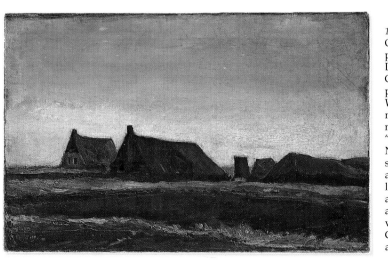

FARMHOUSES
1883; 18 x 22 in (35 x 55.5 cm)
Only a limited number of oil paintings have survived from Drenthe, and it is certain van Gogh abandoned quite a few possessions there on leaving. What remains is elegiac and moving, but these farms are not the primitive, cozy human "nests" he would work from at Nuenen (p. 18); they seem to be stark, forbidding shelters for animals, with no sign of human life. Bleak fenlands are seldom a comforting environment for a dispossessed stranger, but a viewer might wish that van Gogh had painted more of these atmospheric canvases at Drenth

Social realism

When van Gogh was working from the daily life of peasants and artisans at Nuenen, he was not just concerned with conveying a social message about the laborers. Thinking a great deal of certain old masters – he wrote admiringly about Michelangelo – van Gogh was keen to create a "type" representative of many individuals going about their daily tasks. However, he sometimes involuntarily invested the unbeautiful with an aura of the ideal, in his passion to express the truth in nature.

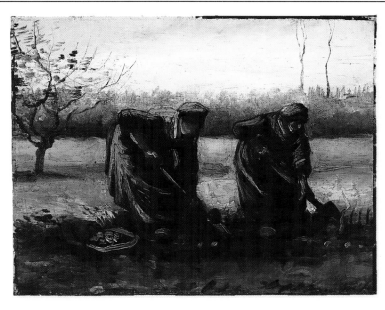

TRADITIONAL WOMAN
Peasant women like this one (above) were as vital as male farmers in the community.

TWO PEASANT WOMEN DIGGING POTATOES
1885; 12½ x 16¾ in (31.5 x 42.5 cm)
Nuenen drawings of work in the fields far outnumber paintings, but there are about half a dozen oils, all of women wearing the coarse blue cloth that van Gogh loved. He wrote to Theo, "The people here instinctively wear the most beautiful blue … when this fades and becomes somewhat discolored by the wind and weather, it is an infinite quiet delicate tone that particularly brings out the flesh colors." In another letter, he comments: "Nothing seems simpler than painting peasants or ragpickers ... but no subjects in painting are as difficult as these commonplace figures."

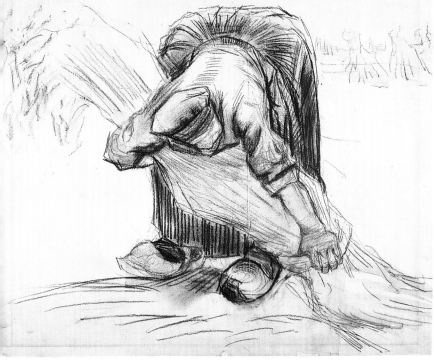

STANDARD FOOTWEAR
Clogs were standard wear for peasants when working in the fields, and for van Gogh they were symbols of the land and simple life.

PEASANT WOMAN BINDING SHEAVES OF CORN
The black chalk drawings that van Gogh made of peasants at work at Nuenen are unequaled graphic accounts of people engaged in hard physical labor. The bold directness of his technique is in accord with the muscular activity being represented. Van Gogh wished to emulate the labors of the peasants himself, and threw himself vigorously into his project of figure studies, writing in May 1885: "If fifty are not enough I shall draw a hundred, and if that is still not enough, even more." During the corn harvest, he worked hard at capturing the reaping, binding and threshing figures, determined to establish his artistic base in the humblest aspects of the real world.

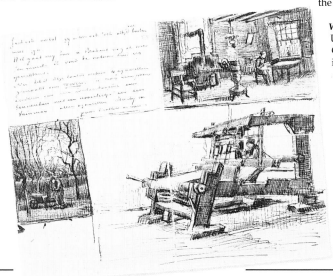

WEAVERS AT WORK
Upon arriving in Nuenen, van Gogh started on a number of works in which weavers were the main subject. Nuenen was part of Brabant, an area in which weaving had always been important, and Vincent felt compelled to illustrate these "Brabant artisans." He wrote to Theo, asking him to show the weaver drawings to other people. He asked Theo to keep the drawings for himself if buyers were not interested. "It would rather disappoint me if you sent these little weavers back to me," he wrote. He valued his work with the weavers very highly.

A love of nature

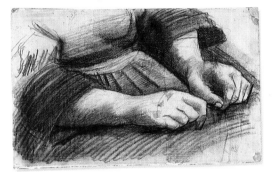

Chaffinch nest

VAN GOGH OFTEN expressed very personal preoccupations in his still life painting. Books, for instance, had personal significance for him. While he was in Nuenen, birds' nests became an important subject, and he paid local boys to find them and bring them to his studio. He found them potent symbols of the maternal and protective, where creatures are born and nurtured. He once referred to the local peasants' cottages as "human nests." Vincent's own domestic dreams were never fulfilled, and it is poignant that he presented his baby nephew with a nest when Theo and Jo brought the child to visit him at Auvers, shortly before he committed suicide (p. 60).

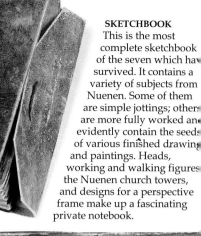

SKETCHBOOK
This is the most complete sketchbook of the seven which have survived. It contains a variety of subjects from Nuenen. Some of them are simple jottings; others are more fully worked and evidently contain the seeds of various finished drawings and paintings. Heads, working and walking figures the Nuenen church towers, and designs for a perspective frame make up a fascinating private notebook.

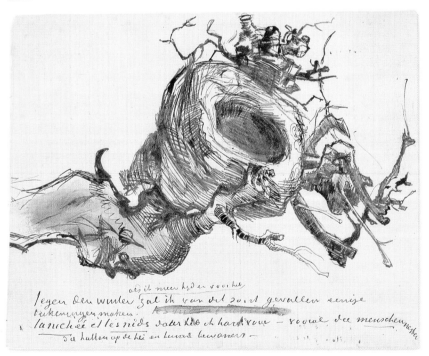

HANDS IN REPOSE
This beautiful and touching child's-eye view of a woman's work-worn hands is one of over 20 known studies of hands made at Nuenen. Van Gogh always conveyed respect for a woman's part in human labor that may have originated in his strong feelings for his hard-working mother.

BIRD'S NEST DRAWING
Vincent sent Theo the vigorous and assured drawing above, probably set up on branches in the studio. "I am now busy painting still lifes of my birds' nests, four of which are finished; I think some people who are good observers of nature might like them because of the colors of the moss, the dry leaves, and the grasses," he wrote.

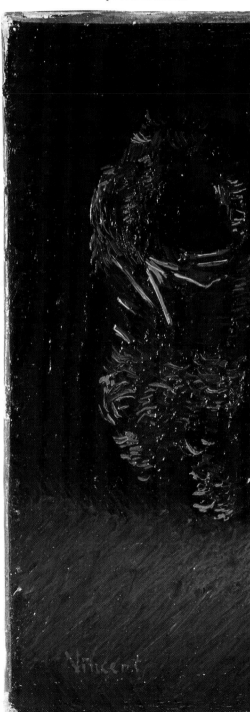

Still Life with Birds' Nests

1885; 13 x 16½ in (33 x 42 cm)

Van Gogh left five paintings of birds' nests which, along with some still lifes with potatoes, are the most monochromatic paintings he ever did. He deliberately painted nests against flat backgrounds because he wanted to make it quite clear that he was not painting them in natural surroundings. He wrote of his reasoning: "A living nest in nature is something quite different; one scarcely sees the nest itself. One sees the birds." Birds would interest him throughout his career.

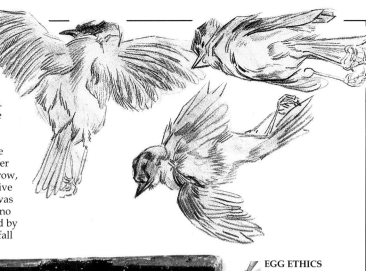

DEAD BIRDS
Birds figured in van Gogh's work as more than just marks to enliven a sky. Later, outside Paris, he would paint a field of wheat transformed by the presence of a single lark. But, in these tender studies of a dead sparrow, arranged with instinctive care on the paper, he was perhaps recalling that no death passes unnoticed by God, who "marks the fall of every sparrow."

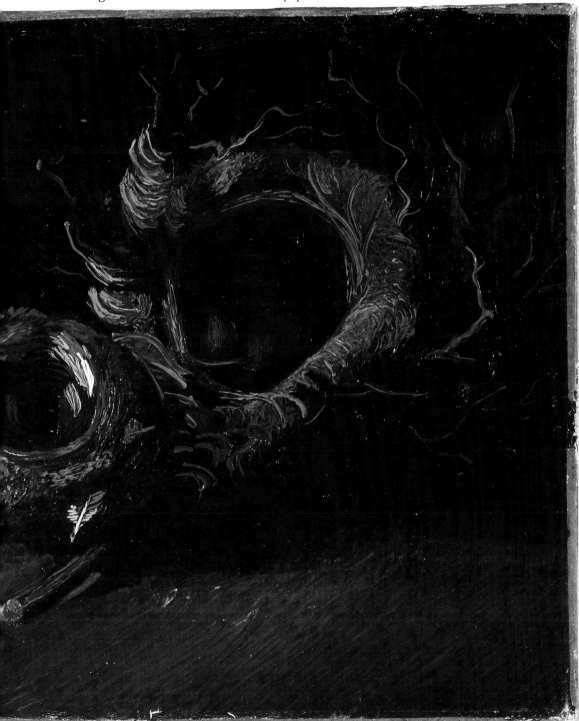

EGG ETHICS
It is not known whether van Gogh allowed the peasant boys to bring him the nests with fertile eggs or whether he only used abandoned ones. To have painted nests without eggs would seem incomplete, though he painted one with just feathers and no eggs, to rather beautiful effect.

TRUE COLOR?
Very little color at all seems to remain in this picture, owing perhaps to van Gogh's use of poor-quality pigments. While in Nuenen, he wrote quite extensively about positive color but seemed shy of lightening his palette, even to perfectly conventional levels.

NEST TYPES
This is one of three birds' nest pictures in which van Gogh used branches to dynamic effect. However, it is clear that they are not painted in their natural setting. From left to right, the nests appear to be those of a long-tailed tit, a chaffinch, and a golden oriole. Van Gogh would certainly have known which birds built each nest.

A matter of faith

THE BIBLE THAT VAN GOGH painted just before leaving home for good, six months after his father's death in 1885, must have meant a great deal to him. Vincent had broken with Christianity – which proved to be one of the most painful experiences of his life, and one from which he never quite recovered. From Arles (p. 42) he would later write with ironic humor of God as an artist whose "study" had not quite succeeded, though it might do so next time. He never came to terms with his loss of faith, particularly as he wished to believe his purpose in life was divinely ordained. Vincent's relationship with his father had been painfully parallel to his obsessive concern with the "meaning" of God and of life itself. Perhaps it was made worse for him in that his liberal father was willing to make considerable allowances for his difficult son.

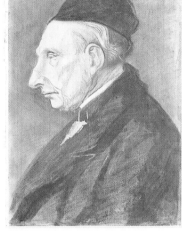

THEODORUS VAN GOGH
1881; 13 x 10 in (33 x 25 cm)
The artist's ambivalence toward his father was central to his emotional conflicts. It cannot have been easy for the respectable pastor to be patient with a son who mixed mainly with local peasants. He merits some sympathy for his battles with his son.

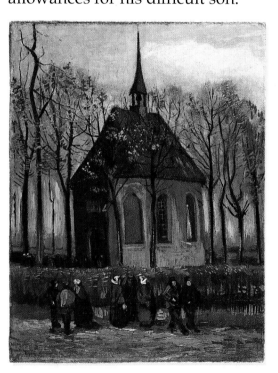

CHURCH AT NUENEN
1884; 16¼ x 12½ in (41.5 x 32 cm)
This is a respectful study of the good folk of Nuenen (p. 17) outside Theodorus's church. But the artist's favorite church was a defunct old tower with an abandoned peasants' graveyard, where he recorded the sale of old crosses. He thought of it when he was painting the church at Auvers in 1890 (p. 59).

HIS FATHER'S BIBLE
The Bible shown here (left) belonged to Theodorus van Gogh. He was confirmed as a minister at Groot Zundert by his clergyman father, who was also called Vincent, in April 1849. Three of Theodorus's brothers became art dealers, and this rather odd family chemistry must have helped determine young Vincent's character. Vincent painted his father's Bible alongside a well-thumbed copy of Emile Zola's novel *Joie de Vivre*, but the artist certainly never attained his own *joie de vivre*.

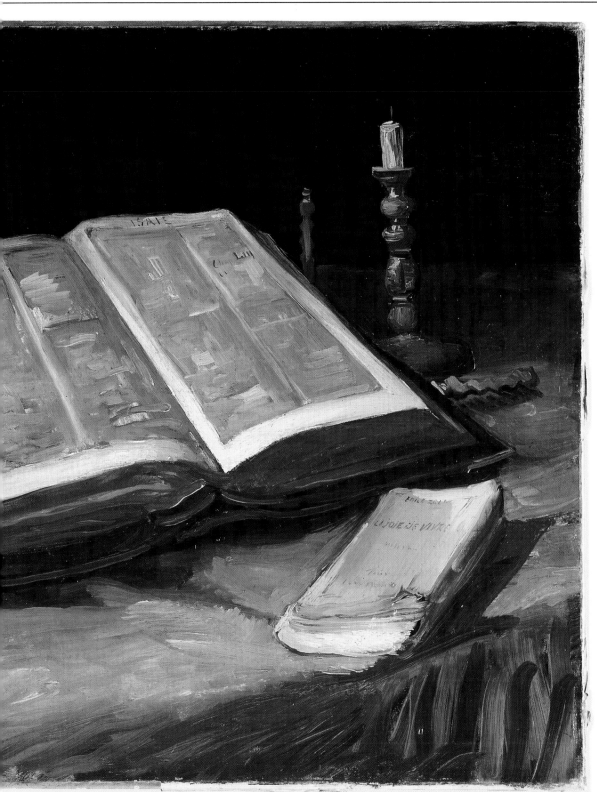

SYMBOLISM
The burned-out candle is certainly a symbol of the transitory nature of life. However, the light on both books seems heaven-sent. (The Bible, for no certain reason, is open at the book of Isaiah.)

COLOR SCHEME
Touches of blue on the Bible and candle lift the picture out of monochrome, as does the reddish brown and the significant yellow of the novel, a color that signified life to van Gogh. Regardless of any meaning, it is a very strong painting.

JOIE DE VIVRE
Though Zola's novel is a bright symbol of liberty against the oppressive Old Testament, the larger book seems the more securely placed, as the smaller one riskily dares the chasm beyond the table's edge. But such symbolism may not have been intended.

WELL-THUMBED
While the pages of the Bible look clean and well cared for, the novel, a cheap and fragile French paperback, looks dog-eared and bent, probably from being carried around in van Gogh's pocket.

Open Bible, Extinguished Candle, and Novel

1885; 25½ x 30¾ in (65 x 78 cm)

This is van Gogh's memorial to his father, a painting that mixes reverence with reproach for the man he had never quite been able to please for the previous ten years. The inclusion of Emile Zola's *Joie de Vivre* is a rebellious symbol against what he saw as his father's outdated views, though there is also respect for the solemn gravity of the Bible. But "I painted that in a rush, in one day," he wrote, not suggesting any significance in the subject matter.

THEODORUS'S DEATH
This record book shows the entry for Vincent's father's death. Theodorus dropped dead on the threshold of his vicarage after a walk on March 26, 1885. Van Gogh's reaction to the news seemed curiously neutral.

A peasant meal

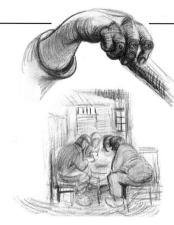

AT NUENEN VAN GOGH GAVE active physical toil an unprecedented reality. Its impact went far beyond anything the realist Gustave Courbet had achieved, beyond even the quasi-religious images of Jean-François Millet (p. 12). He made a number of studies of peasant hands and heads before embarking on what would be his most important piece of work at Nuenen. The pinnacle of his work in Holland was *The Potato Eaters*, a scene painted in April 1885 that shows the working day to be over and the peasants enjoying the humble fruits of their labor. Van Gogh counted it among his very best, and with its complex narrative detail it demands a different kind of scrutiny than his other pictures of peasant life. Never in art had respect for labor been quite so imaginatively conveyed.

PREPARATORY WORK
The earliest germ of the idea for *The Potato Eaters* included a powerful hand. There were further sketches, two oil studies of the composition, and a lithograph – plus numerous studies of heads and hands.

DARK PALETTE
Van Gogh's palette was influenced by the cost and availability of painting materials, as well as the bleak Nuenen landscape. The greenish colors used in this painting could never have appealed to the art dealers of Paris. Van Gogh wanted the canvas to be displayed in a gold or copper frame, or against golden wallpaper, to echo his painted highlights.

Black   Olive green   Raw umber   Pale ochre   Raw sienna

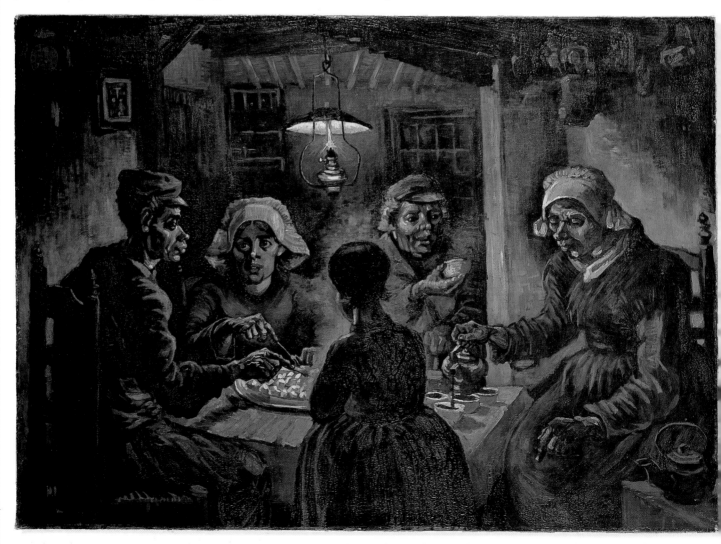

ATMOSPHERIC LIGHTING

The oil lamp is not quite central in the painting, but it is certainly a central symbol – both a light and a focal point. It gives the entire scene the atmosphere of a nativity, and the orange streaks of paint supply an essential touch of warmth to the picture. The dark silhouette of the girl's back provides a center of gravity, and the tentatively painted steam from the potatoes creates a halo around her. This is one of the rare occasions when van Gogh created a soft, atmospheric effect.

Strong, dark shadows convey the feel of the fabric

THE OUTSIDER

This plump peasant is a decidedly different character from the other male, eating his meal with little sense of ceremony. Although central, he does seem a little detached from the "communion." Van Gogh's brushstrokes are therefore gentler here; he seems less anxious to find expressive detail. There is no doubt that van Gogh saw all five human subjects as the people he knew well, and he does not rob them of their individuality.

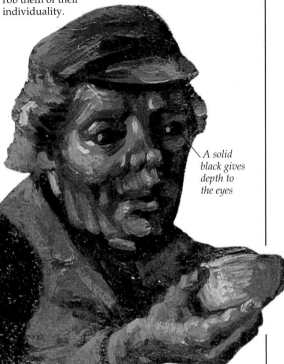

A solid black gives depth to the eyes

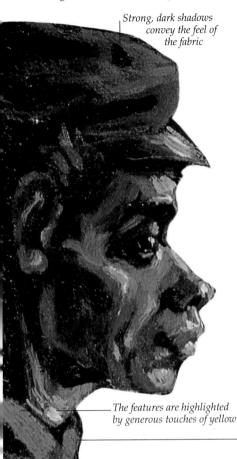

The features are highlighted by generous touches of yellow

WORK-WORN HANDS

The gnarled hands, with their protruding veins, stop just short of the grotesque. Van Gogh drew hands wonderfully at Nuenen, but the exaggeration here is deliberate, since they are of paramount symbolic importance. Not only the color, but also the kind of brushstroke used, contrasts the instruments of labor with its fruits, which are firmly painted in glowing chunks. The artist's obstinate resistance to an unnecessary refinement with the brush was the aspect of his work that Theo seemed to find the most troubling.

TWISTED PROFILE

Van Gogh paints, like Rembrandt, from flat dark to impasted light. The background color, with its subtle modulations of gray, blue, and brown, is also similar to the method of Rembrandt in being dark and difficult to name. This man (above) is probably Cornelius de Groot, seated next to his sister. The twists and angles of his body have been exaggerated to emphasize physical stresses, and his mouth has been turned to the side of the natural profile to establish his likeness.

An evocation of muscle and veins by simple strokes

Summary square strokes define the potatoes

The Potato Eaters

1885; 32¼ x 45 in (82 x 114 cm)

"I have tried to emphasize that these people, eating their potatoes in the lamplight, have dug the earth with those very hands they put in the dish, and so it speaks of manual labor and how they have honestly earned their food." This is probably the most considered picture van Gogh ever painted. Many studies of heads, hands, and of the composition itself led up to it, and he became entirely immersed. "I have such a feel of the thing that I can literally dream it, " he wrote.

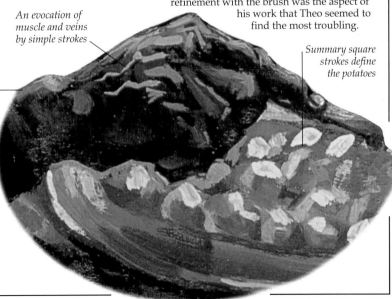

Arrival in Antwerp

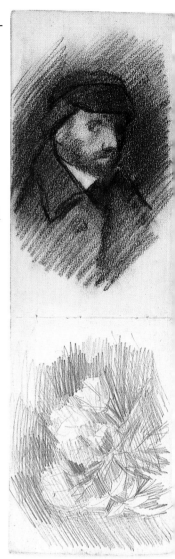

VAN GOGH WENT TO ANTWERP in November 1885, partly to escape local gossip concerning himself and a peasant girl, but mainly to find new subject matter, including, he hoped, the nude. His great labors at Nuenen had prepared him well, and his desire to meet other artists might at last be realized in Antwerp. His first letters from there describe the paintings he saw and the cosmopolitan life of the city. He vainly attempted to make money from painting portraits, townscapes, and tradesmen's signs, then enrolled at the Antwerp Academy to make use of the life-class models. Shortage of money led to van Gogh's undernourishment and acute physical distress.

ANTWERP HOME
Van Gogh rented a room at 194 Rue des Images and decorated it with Japanese prints.

ACADEMY CARD
Several weeks after his arrival in Antwerp, van Gogh submitted five of his paintings to the Academy and was duly admitted. He was simply looking for affordable, live models to work from, but was amazed to find that he liked drawing from the antique plaster casts there.

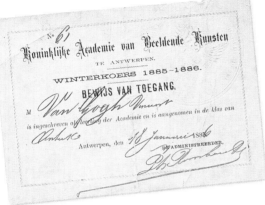

EARLY SELF-PORTRAIT
This rather poor drawing (top right) expresses van Gogh's occasionally very low spirits in Antwerp only too well. It is one of a very similar pair and has been identified as a self-portrait. This is not quite certain, but if so it is an extraordinarily poor begining to a series that, when completed, would approach the significance of Rembrandt's extensive series of self-portraits.

GROOTMARKT DRAWING
A few drawings of the streets and buildings of Antwerp survive – this one of the Grootmarkt (left), two of the Kastel Het Steen, and a sketch of the Church of Our Lady. There are also a few of street life, a painting of the backs of some houses, and one of a quay with ships, but nothing that seems quite worthy of the great draftsman-painter of Nuenen.

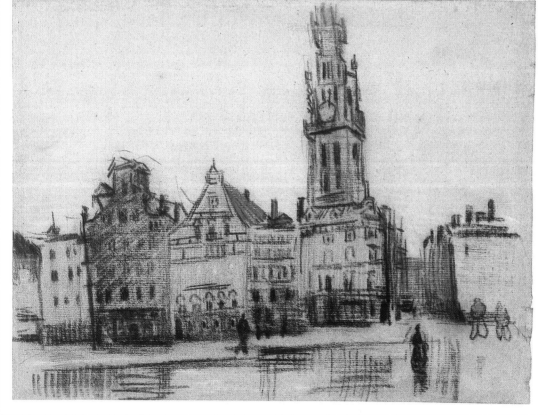

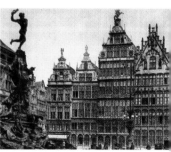

ANTWERP GROOTMARKT
This is the main square and former market (*markt*) place of Belgium's great port and commercial center, which lies on the border with Holland. Van Gogh liked the vigorous life of the city, and later even thought of returning there.

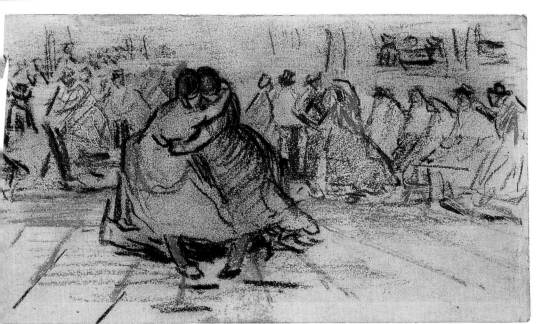

DANCE HALL DRAWING
Van Gogh described a sailors' ball in Antwerp to Theo – how he was struck by everyone behaving "quite decently," and how they were neither drunk nor drinking too much. He enthused about the great atmosphere of enjoyment and proceeded to draw the spectacle it presented. Two drawings of dance halls survive, and they are reminiscent of the graphic images of Toulouse-Lautrec, who was only just beginning to immerse himself in the dance halls and cabarets of Paris. Although van Gogh had not yet seen any of his work, they would soon meet in Paris (p. 28).

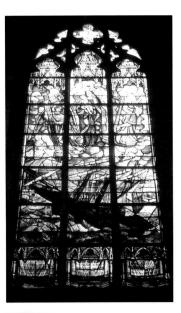

STAINED GLASS
This window, called the *Maris Stella* (Star of the Sea), is in the St. Andrieskerk, Antwerp, and it greatly impressed van Gogh. He had used the symbolism of ships (their wreck and salvage) to describe his personal predicament in several of his letters, and it is no wonder that this simple 16th-century design, with its unpretentious form and color, appealed to him.

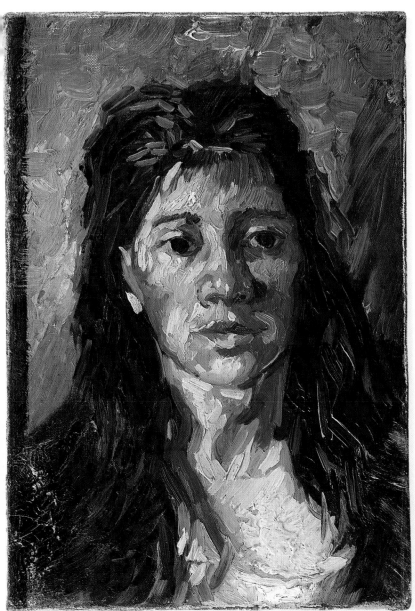

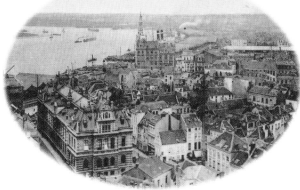

CITY ON A RIVER
Antwerp's townscape and boats on the River Schelde (above) were painted by van Gogh, although few of these works survive.

WOMAN WITH HER HAIR LOOSE
1885; 13¾ x 9½ in (32 x 24 cm)
Van Gogh found the girls of Antwerp handsome, but commented that the most beautiful were "plain faced … with an ugly or irregular face, but lively and piquant *à la* Frans Hals." As he became interested in Rubens' work, with his painting of heads and hands with "streaks of pure red," van Gogh's flesh tints grew warmer. But he rejected Rubens' flowing strokes, remaining faithful to the coarser brushwork of Frans Hals.

The Antwerp Academy

WHEN VAN GOGH ENROLLED at the Academy in Antwerp in January 1886, he had just finished drawings that would one day be compared to the old masters. Although willing to learn, he astonished fellow students by refusing to abandon the rapidity and boldness of his own methods. There is no doubt that unfamiliar circumstances, and the humility that went with his willful pride, put him off his stride and produced some disappointing results. He was, in fact, downgraded to the beginners' class just as he left for Paris, but he probably never knew of this humiliation. Antwerp was both a trough and a watershed for van Gogh.

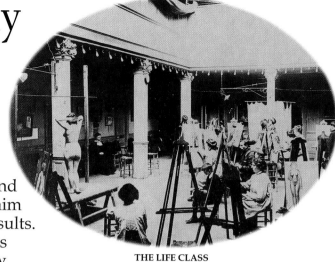

THE LIFE CLASS
The life room was a step beyond the antique class and the high temple of draftsmanship. A single drawing could take days, a pace that van Gogh, only patient working at speed, would have found entirely unnatural.

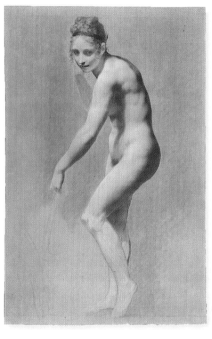

PRUD'HON DRAWING
This life drawing by Pierre Paul Prud'hon (left) is in the style taught at the Academy. It is nothing like van Gogh's robust approach. He believed in what Eugène Delacroix is reputed to have said: "The ancients did not tackle it from the contour but from the center." The Antwerp Academy would not tolerate modeling before the contour was established, and van Gogh's deliberate defiance of the rules was asking for his teacher's rejection.

Charcoal

Conté

CHARCOAL AND CRAYON
Van Gogh favored black crayon or charcoal for his drawings. Theo once sent him some crayon, and his brother wrote back with the response, "that crayon is what I want; it listens with intelligence and obeys … that crayon has a real gypsy soul…."

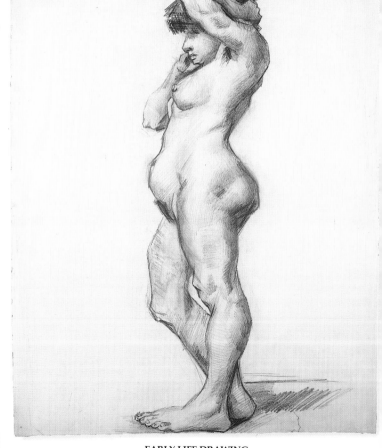

EARLY LIFE DRAWING
This rather awkward and ill-proportioned drawing nevertheless carries the stamp of a draftsman through its attack and presence. Van Gogh seems to have coarsened the model's physical features, giving her huge feet and failing with her right leg completely. Though he had been able to convey a strong sense of the body under clothes, when laid bare it must have seemed a problem. In his previous figure drawing he had been accustomed to the form-shaping folds and edges of clothes, complex facial features, and surface markings. His only previous nude, "Sorrow," (p. 14) used little modeling, and smooth white skin was foreign to him.

Skull with Cigarette

1885; 12¾ x 9½ in (32.5 x 24 cm)

This harrowing picture was probably painted from a skeleton used in the anatomy class, and it cannot but make the viewer think of van Gogh's bad health at this time. While in Antwerp he was reportedly diagnosed as having syphilis, and his teeth were rotting, damaging a stomach that never had enough food in it. The image seems a defiant complaint against his condition, but it is perhaps the most assured painting he did in Antwerp.

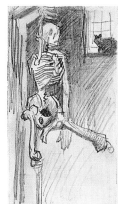

SKELETON DRAWING
This is a seemingly humorous sketch of a skeleton from the Academy. Van Gogh never produced his greatest works in pencil. Remarks to Theo show how much he depended on his choice of drawing materials to inspire him.

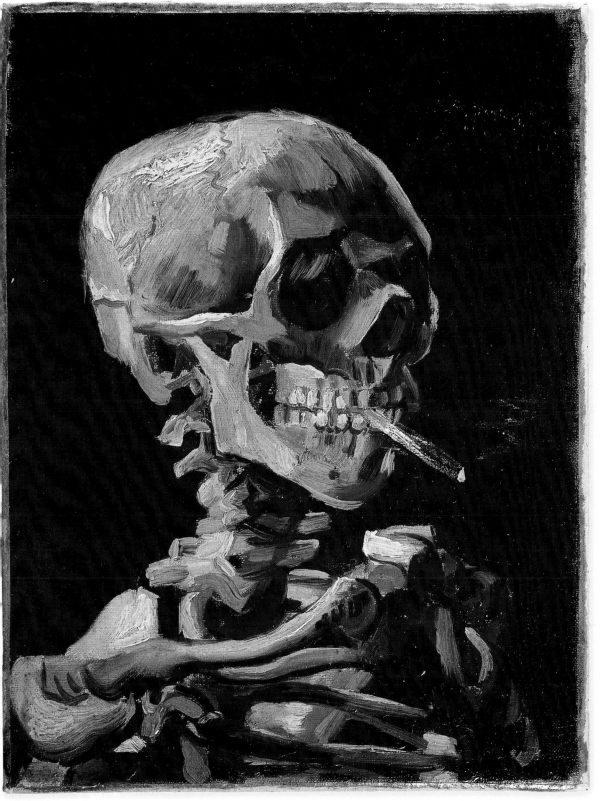

MORBID IMAGERY
Van Gogh may have been influenced by the Belgian artist Felicien Rops and his often-morbid subject matter.

THE CIGARETTE
Van Gogh evidently declined to lend the skeleton his beloved pipe. Instead, he placed a cigarette between the skull's teeth. It is possibly an afterthought, and it is quite likely that he kept the picture partly as a souvenir of his acute malaise.

WELL OBSERVED
Even in this troubling image, van Gogh conveys, with the energy of an electrical charge, how closely and quickly he has observed the subject. Although he ignores odd imperfections in the application of paint, this work illustrates how misleading reports of his wildness at the easel were.

DUTCH CONNECTION
A 17th-century Dutch artist, Hercules Segers, painted a similarly powerful skull. It is not certain that van Gogh knew his work, but interesting affinities have been noted between the two.

A Parisian experience

VAN GOGH ARRIVED unannounced in Paris in March 1886; Theo had not expected him until June. "Don't be cross for my coming all at once like this," he wrote anxiously in a note sent from the station. Moving in with Theo, who would be obliged to find a larger apartment, he started work as soon as he could, sketching outside and working at the studio of Fernand Cormon. He made several good friends in Paris, and even gained admirers, but as a man and a painter, the general view of him was that he was mentally unstable. Van Gogh was considered good-hearted but also argumentative and stubborn – often testing Theo's patience. After only a few months, Vincent left Cormon's studio and declared that he felt more "himself." He needed two years of freedom and experimentation to find his true path.

THE MOULIN ROUGE
This photograph captures the mood of Paris in the late 19th century. Dancers, actors, and artists traveled to the city to display their skills, as Paris aspired to become the cultural capital of the world.

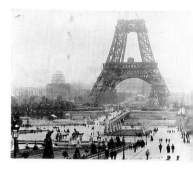

THE EIFFEL TOWER
At the time of van Gogh's arrival, the Eiffel Tower was being built for the Universal Exhibition of 1889. The exhibition celebrated France's technical and scientific achievements.

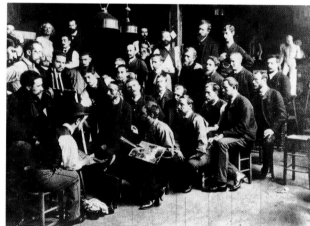

CORMON'S STUDIO
Van Gogh worked at the studio for three or four months and, although he impressed his fellow students, he did not produce work of any real quality. Henri de Toulouse-Lautrec (seated left) and Emile Bernard (top right) can be seen in the group photo; the latter became one of van Gogh's best painter friends.

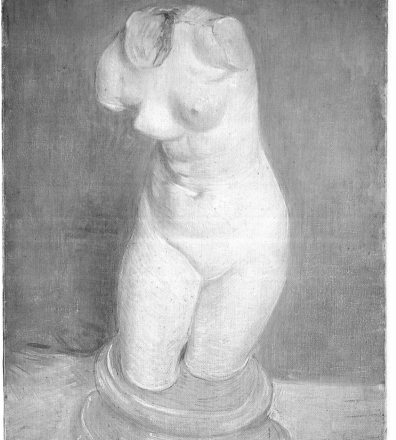

PLASTER STATUETTE
1886; 16 x 13 in (41 x 32.5 cm)
This plaster statuette (right) was owned by van Gogh. He painted another (left) at Cormon's studio, and it is one of several works that have survived from the period. A few paintings betray the wild methods of execution reported by van Gogh's fellow students, but this one conveys care and a hint of tenderness. There are experimental touches of crimson in the shadows, along with the overall blue. Paintings of casts were once common, but few have survived. Bernard ironically recollected van Gogh's brief struggle with the plaster casts at Cormon's, saying that he worked "with angelic patience," but nevertheless wore a hole in the paper with his eraser.

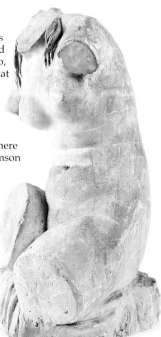

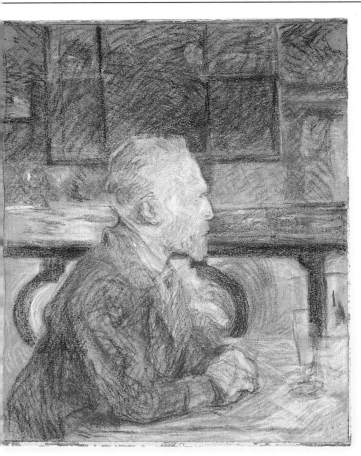

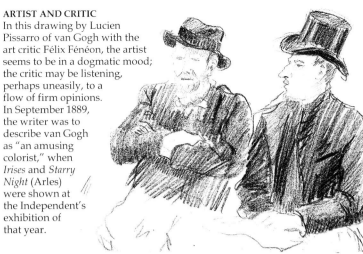

ARTIST AND CRITIC
In this drawing by Lucien Pissarro of van Gogh with the art critic Félix Fénéon, the artist seems to be in a dogmatic mood; the critic may be listening, perhaps uneasily, to a flow of firm opinions. In September 1889, the writer was to describe van Gogh as "an amusing colorist," when *Irises* and *Starry Night* (Arles) were shown at the Independent's exhibition of that year.

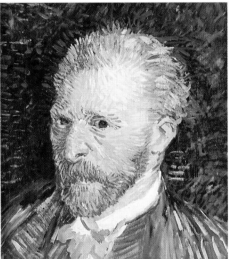

SELF-PORTRAIT
1887; 18½ x 13¾ in (47 x 35 cm)
Van Gogh's self-portraits in Paris were, in part, painterly exercises, using himself as a readily available model. They also represent a dialogue with himself, from the uncertain artist adopting a sober black hat to the exhausted but assured veteran of nearly two years later. Van Gogh made at least 28 self-images there, and this early one could be seen as an untroubled exercise in likeness.

VINCENT VAN GOGH
Henri de Toulouse-Lautrec; 1886; 21¼ x 17¾ in (53 x 44 cm)
This pastel is a sympathetic image of van Gogh in Paris. Toulouse-Lautrec's work later showed van Gogh's influence, but it is not clear how close their relationship was. It was once suggested that Lautrec encouraged van Gogh to go south because he was tired of the Dutchman, but there is no proof of this.

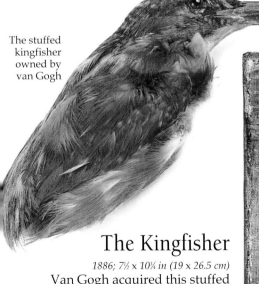

The stuffed kingfisher owned by van Gogh

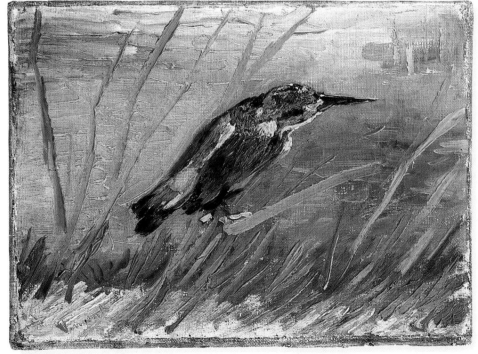

The Kingfisher

1886; 7½ x 10¼ in (19 x 26.5 cm)
Van Gogh acquired this stuffed kingfisher (above) in Paris and painted it as if it were alive, in a natural setting. From another artist this might have been an embarrassing work, but van Gogh could convey a sense of life in painting, even when working as carelessly as this. It shows a touching nostalgia for his youthful interest in the countryside.

Images of Paris

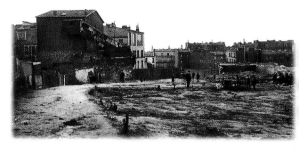

BECAUSE VINCENT'S correspondence with Theo ceased when he arrived in Paris, we know less of van Gogh's feelings about his work during his stay in the city than about the rest of his painting career. In Antwerp, he had been looking for a new start after his considerable achievements in Holland. The results had been unsatisfactory, but there could be no turning back. In Paris, he was subject to a bewildering variety of ideas, and his intelligence and instinct would sort them all out only with time. His first works in Paris seem subdued and tentative, but only in comparison with his confidence in Holland and the certainty he would gain in the south. His modesty was real, but always outweighed by a belief in himself that even van Gogh must sometimes have found surprising.

THE HILL OF MONTMARTRE
Four months after arriving in Paris, van Gogh moved to an apartment below Montmartre with Theo. The area, covered with smallholdings and windmills, would soon be transformed into an artists' quarter as Paris expanded.

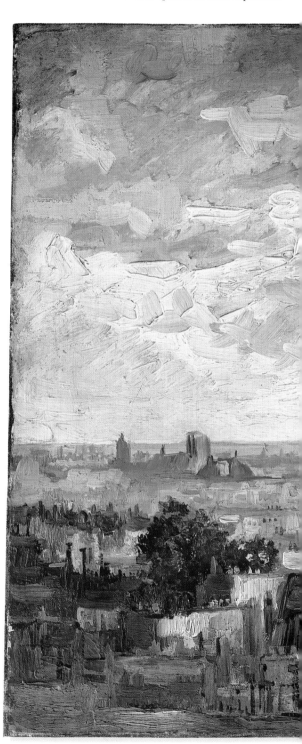

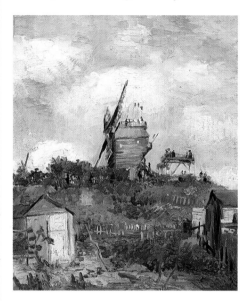

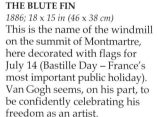

RURAL PARIS
Montmartre before the Sacre Coeur was completed in 1919.

THE BLUTE FIN
1886; 18 x 15 in (46 x 38 cm)
This is the name of the windmill on the summit of Montmartre, here decorated with flags for July 14 (Bastille Day – France's most important public holiday). Van Gogh seems, on his part, to be confidently celebrating his freedom as an artist.

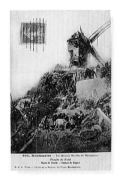

**SELF-PORTRAIT
WITH DARK FELT HAT**
1886; 16 x 13 in (41 x 32.5 cm)
Van Gogh's first self-portrait conveys an anxious, and perhaps experimental, dignity of a man who does not know how he should look and dress as an artist in Paris. He seems to be asking to be taken seriously - a different man than the one who was so uncertain in the city ten years earlier. This was the first self-portrait van Gogh painted in Paris.

The Roofs of Paris

1886; 21¼ x 28½ in (54 x 72 cm)

This view from Montmartre was one of several paintings and sketches van Gogh made from above the city within two months of his arrival. It was a remarkably successful approach to an entirely new subject. The distance is beautifully realized and the at first impulsive-looking *impasto* of the sky seems more and more well conceived as the viewer looks at it. It is likely that while painting this picture, van Gogh thought of the landscape artist, Camille Corot, and his "values," one of which was to judge finely the tonalities of a motif.

GUINGUETTE IN MONTMARTRE
1886; 19½ x 25½ in (49.5 x 64.5 cm)
A *guinguette* was a cheap suburban outdoor café, and this one was in the suburb of Montmartre. Painted in the early autumn, this work is little more than a sketch, but both memorable and evocative. It is partly Impressionist, but it has long linear strokes reminiscent of Manet's; the latticework is also suggestive of Japanese calligraphy. Van Gogh was now absorbing a formidable and varied number of artistic ideas.

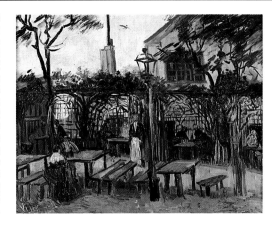

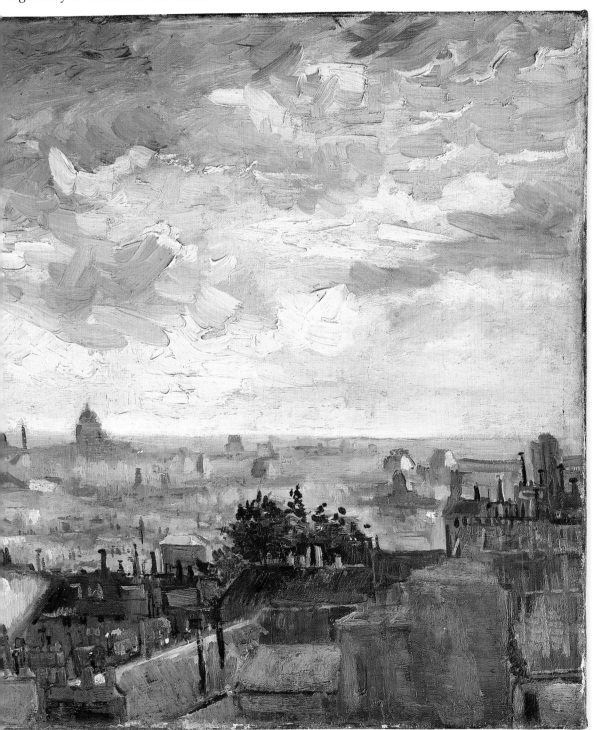

IMPOSING SKY
The sky is applied with calculated boldness, not in a spirit of exaggeration or Expressionism, but simply to establish its value as van Gogh saw it. Neither is it particularly Impressionist. The whole picture is a natural synthesis of what van Gogh had already taught himself and of what he was learning in Paris.

ATMOSPHERE
The distance and middle distance are brushed on smoothly with little tonal contrast. Traces of brown-red accent the blue-gray, as in the sky. The city seems to be under a light haze of coal smoke from which the Pantheon (center) and Nôtre Dame cathedral emerge.

FOREGROUND
The foreground is much more sharply defined than the rest of the picture, with the foliage and chimney pots strongly accented. There seems to be some sienna underpainting in the foreground, but not over all.

OPTICAL SKILL
The eye is compelled down into the city in the center. As an unaccustomed attempt at rendering varying visibility, the painting is certainly a brilliant success.

The Impressionists

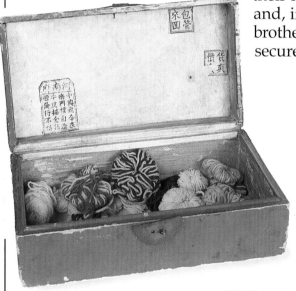

VASE OF FLOWERS
Adolphe Monticelli; 1880;
20 x 15¼ in (51 x 39 cm)
Monticelli, one of van Gogh's
greatest heroes, exerted a strong
influence on his work.

Iɴ Pᴀʀɪs, van Gogh was soon confronted with
an extraordinary variety of paintings, a number
of which, including works by Monet, Theo had
been trying to promote through his employers,
Boussod and Valadon. Vincent referred to them
all as Impressionists, although many were
known as Neo-Impressionists. He soon joined
in Theo's struggle on their behalf, and his
brother later acknowledged the important role
Vincent had played in creating a circle of artists
and friends from which they both benefited,
even if not materially. Vincent's absorption of
their ideas was remarkably wide-ranging
and, if he often put a great strain on his
brother, his intelligence and warm heart
secured Theo's respect and affection.

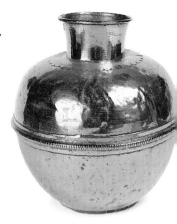

COPPER VASE
This is the actual round copper
vase used by van Gogh in his
Fritillarias painting (below).

THE USE OF WOOLS
Van Gogh owned this
Japanese lacquered box
(above) while in Paris
and kept these knots
of colored wool inside.
They were used to
make up combinations
of complementary
colors (p. 63) –
important to an artist
who was experimenting
with the use of color.
Van Gogh became a
colorist, late-arrived
but bolder than many.

FRITILLARIAS
1887; 29 x 24 in (73.5 x 60.5 cm)
Van Gogh's first series of
flower pieces in Paris seem
influenced more by Monticelli
than his own contemporaries.
In 1887, he gave this painting a
pointillist (p. 34) background,
and a somewhat Impressionist
vase, though shaped by his
own brand of drawing with
the brush. It is a masterful,
apparently spontaneous,
performance and it conveys
the unique sense of rapid
application over all.

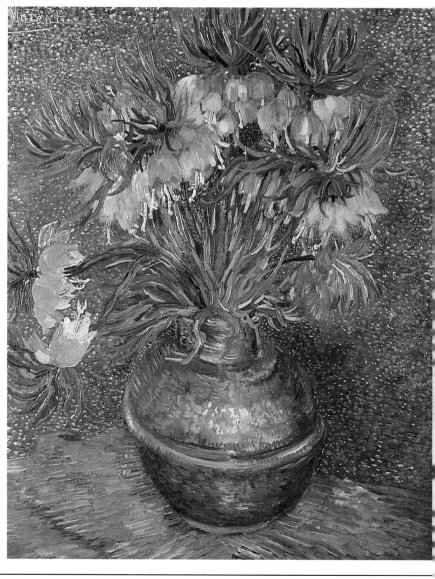

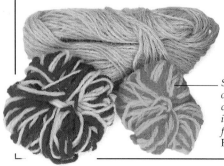

*Some elements
of these color
combinations are
illustrated in the
flower blooms of*
Fritillarias *(right)*

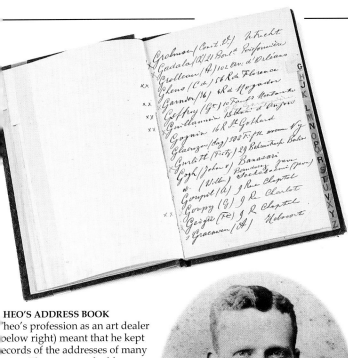

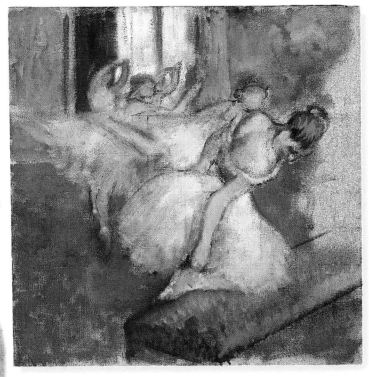

BALLET DANCERS
Edgar Degas; 1880; 27 x 27½ in (72 x 73 cm)
Van Gogh must have seen Degas's famous series of nude pastels at the 1886 Impressionist Exhibition in Paris, and he told Emile Bernard that he found "calm perfection" in his work. Gauguin claimed van Gogh detested the master, but van Gogh, in a letter, only once mocked Degas.

HEO'S ADDRESS BOOK
heo's profession as an art dealer
below right) meant that he kept
ecords of the addresses of many
rtists. The names and addresses
f Paul Gauguin, and the early
mpressionist, Armand
Guillaumin, are clearly visible.

HE NOBLE BROTHER
Theo van Gogh was a noble
pirit, but his doubts about his
rother's worth as a painter created
owerful tensions between them. The
urvival of their "collaboration" while
haring an apartment in Paris showed
emarkable forbearance on both their parts.

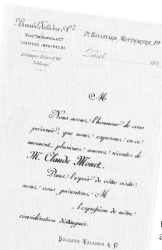

MONET EXHIBITION
As manager of one of the galleries of Boussod and Valadon, Theo was quite influential in Parisian art circles. He organized an exhibition for Monet (left) at his gallery in the Boulevard Montmartre. For a time, Theo worked as a dealer for Monet, as well as for Camille Pissarro, Degas, and Gauguin.

THE ORIGINAL IMPRESSIONIST
Claude Monet was one of the "purest" Impressionists; his painting *Impression, Sunrise* was used by a hostile journalist to give the movement its name. Van Gogh admired his use of light and color.

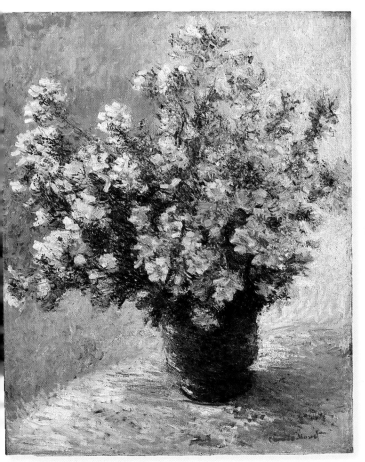

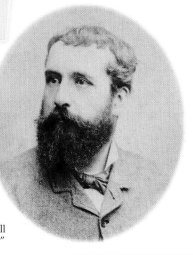

VASE OF FLOWERS
Claude Monet; 1882;
39½ x 32¼ in (100 x 82 cm)
Theo bought 14 paintings from Monet in 1887, and more the following year. This vase of wild mallow was, however, painted in 1882, while van Gogh was struggling with elementary drawing and painting in The Hague. Monet admired van Gogh's work, and after his death, asked, "How could a man who so loved flowers and light, and has rendered them so well ... have managed to be so unhappy?"

New approaches

VAN GOGH ADMIRED the Impressionists (p. 32), and was in their debt for opening up new possibilities for painters, but he was never really one of them. In Paris he met many Neo-Impressionist artists such as Paul Signac, Emile Bernard, and the innovative Georges Seurat (below, left), whose pointillist paintings had been greeted with such acclaim. The abstract element of Seurat's painting appealed

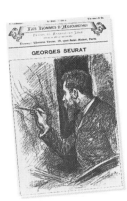

to van Gogh, and elements of his pointillist technique, with the use of pure primary colors applied in separate strokes, dots, and touches, are to be found in *People in a Park at Asnières*. However, while van Gogh was never truly an Impressionist, neither was he ever a pointillist.

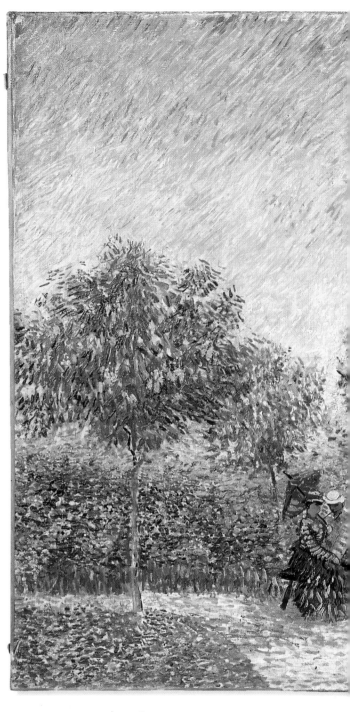

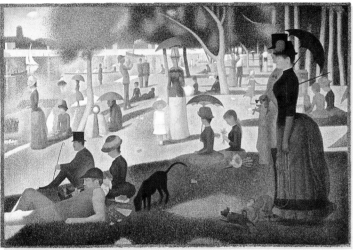

LA GRANDE JATTE
Georges Seurat; 1886;
81 x 120½ in (207.6 x 308 cm)
Seurat's first pointillist work was completed in the spring of 1886, a year before van Gogh's *People in a Park at Asnières*. Seurat started by making several sketches outdoors using an Impressionist technique, but began to experiment as he worked. The result was a painting composed of small dots of pure color, designed to be mixed in the eye of the observer. It was presented to great acclaim from some, but it also divided opinion in the art world. Van Gogh's picture no doubt refers to *La Grand Jatte*, but he was not attempting to match it in his much smaller, more lyrical work.

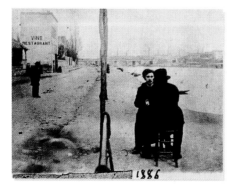

POSITIVELY VAN GOGH
One of only three existing photographs of the artist, seen from the back in conversation with Emile Bernard in Asnières, Paris, in 1886.

People in a Park at Asnières

1887; 29½ x 44¼ in (75 x 112.5 cm)
This picture is a joyous celebration of complementary colors, of spring, and of love. Van Gogh wrote of "colors ... which marry each other ... complement each other as a man and woman do. " He wrote to Theo, away in Holland, about such wide canvases being "... too difficult to sell, but later on people will see that there is open air in them, and good humor...." The picture was exhibited in the rehearsal room of a Paris theater, where Seurat and his follower Paul Signac also showed.

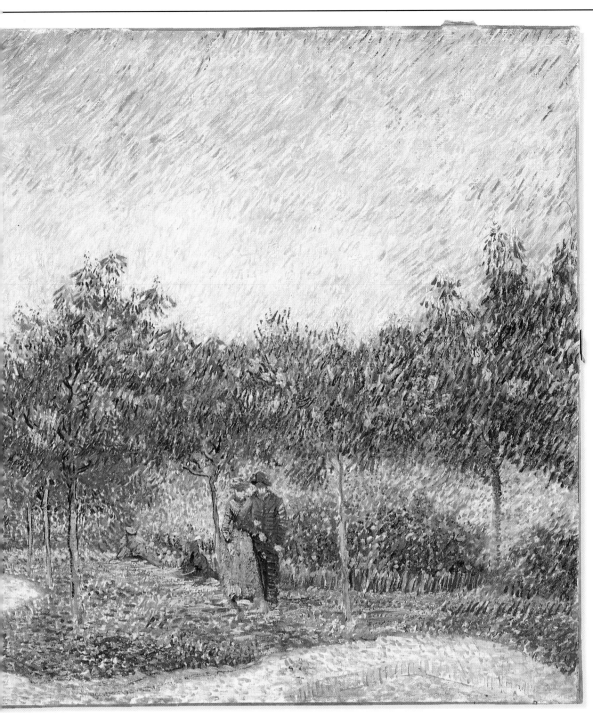

SKY COLORS
For the sky, van Gogh used slanted blue strokes on a white ground, which gives the sense of light falling like rain. There are yellow touches above the foliage. The only other skies he painted with so little color variation as this were in one or two landscapes in Arles, two years later.

FOLIAGE
The trees offer their shade to the lovers in the late spring sunshine. The pink and red chestnut blossom accentuate the green in the painting, adding some warmth to the composition.

RELATIONSHIPS
Since his time in Antwerp, van Gogh had shown an interest in couples. They seem to represent an ideal human harmony.

LOVERS' PATHS
Van Gogh often used the compositional and symbolic devices provided by paths, roads, and tracks. Here the paths seem simply to be offering the lovers a variety of pleasant walks.

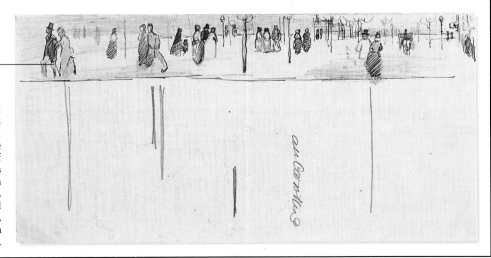

This rapid sketch recalls van Gogh's old ambition to be a graphic artist

MENU SKETCH
When van Gogh first arrived in Paris, the subjects immediately available to him were the streets and open spaces of the city. This sketch was made on the border of a café menu and is probably of a scene visible from his table – where he was no doubt feeling better fed than he had been in Antwerp. It was composed in pencil, plus violet and black ink. Van Gogh would draw at any opportunity, on scraps of paper, letters, books – whatever was available when he felt inspired to sketch the scene before him.

Japanese influences

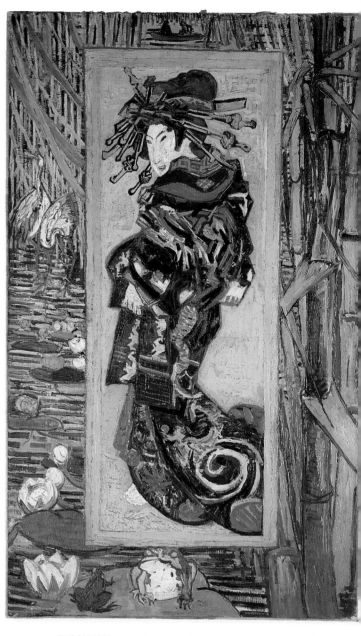

"JAPONISME," the influence of Japan on Western art, had been beguiling Europe for about 30 years when, in Antwerp, van Gogh first discovered the thousands of Japanese prints available. "My studio is not so bad, especially as I have pinned a lot of little Japanese prints on the wall, which amuse me very much," he announced to Theo. But it was in Paris that Japanese art influenced him enormously. Without the example of Japan, van Gogh's *oeuvre* would have looked very different – and perhaps not quite so extraordinary. Ignoring the art's exotic and erotic charms, he was influenced much more by its outlined areas of even color and its evocation of the serene union between humanity and nature.

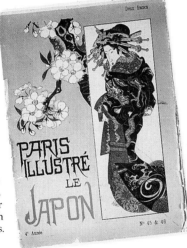

PARIS ILLUSTRE COVER
This popular magazine, which van Gogh copied (right), confirms the popularity of "Japonaiserie" in Paris by using a print by Keisai Eisen on the cover. Prints, ceramics, furniture, fashions, and gardens all reflected the influence of a country which, unlike China, had only been open to the West for about 50 years when van Gogh bought his first Japanese prints.

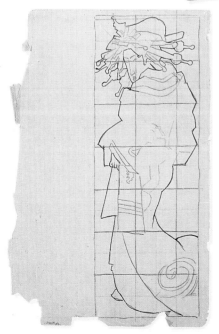

SQUARED-UP PRINT
Van Gogh squared up the magazine cover in order to double its size on canvas. He would use the same conventional method for transferring engravings from Millet and others onto canvas at St. Rémy (pp. 52–53). The craze for "Japonisme" was reflected in Impressionist art 15 years previously in the painting of Manet's *Nina de Callias,* 1873, then in Monet's *La Japonaise,* where a French woman is arrayed in spectacular Japanese costume. The works of Degas and Renoir also feature Japanese objects and style.

JAPONAISERIE: THE COURTESAN (AFTER KEISAI EISEN)
1887; 41¼ x 24 in (105 x 60.5 cm)
For van Gogh, it was the spirit and form of Japanese art that mattered, particularly its flat, pure colors. His Japonaiseries were exercises he must have enjoyed. Here, he made Eisen's figure into a framed picture, hanging in front of a three-dimensional background, and added motifs from other prints – a boat, reeds, frogs, and cranes. The names of the creatures shown (frogs and cranes) were French slang terms for prostitutes – a joke referring to the Japanese courtesan depicted.

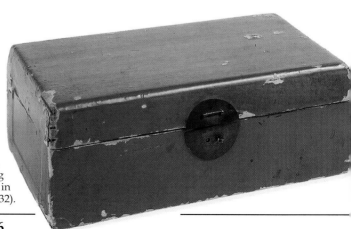

RED LACQUERED BOX
Van Gogh's interest in Japan extended as far as owning this Japanese box (right), in which wools were kept (p. 32).

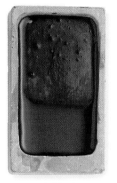
Ink block

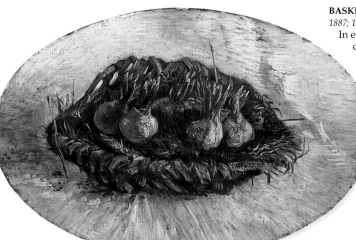

BASKET WITH SPROUTING BULBS
1887; 13 x 19 in (31.5 x 48 cm)
In early 1887, van Gogh used the oval lids of two rough Japanese boxes on which to paint still lifes. Here he exploited the shape in a very satisfying way, depicting a basket with bulbs on the lid (left). On the lid of the other box, he painted three novels – the reverse of this lid is shown below, revealing its origins. He took visible pleasure in symbols of life renewed and life well recorded. In his famous canvas *Chair with Pipe* (p. 44), van Gogh was even to incorporate sprouting bulbs by his signature.

Reed pen

THE ART OF DRAWING
Van Gogh came to favor both the steel and the reed pen for drawing. The reed had been in use for centuries in both East and West. He would emulate the qualities of Japanese woodcuts with them, and sometimes, in paintings, would evoke oriental calligraphy with the brush. He once asked Theo to make up some folding albums of his drawings in the Japanese manner (below), though perhaps his greatest tribute to Japan was to paint himself as a Buddhist priest.

Original Japanese calligraphy

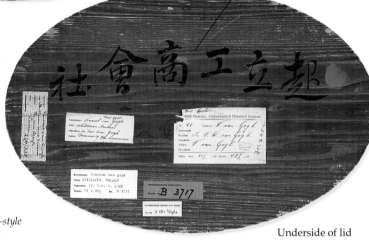

Underside of lid

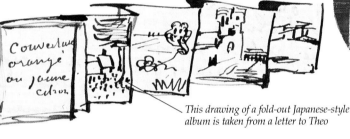

This drawing of a fold-out Japanese-style album is taken from a letter to Theo

PERE TANGUY
1888; 36¾ x 29 in (93 x 74 cm)
Père Tanguy, the art supplier, helped promote many artists' works and was one of van Gogh's few committed admirers in Paris. As a measure of his affection, van Gogh painted two portraits of him. The background of Japanese prints represents the more just world that Tanguy, a socialist, so passionately desired.

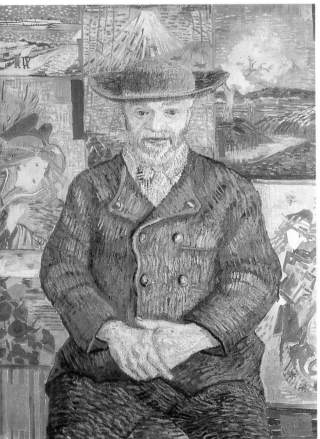

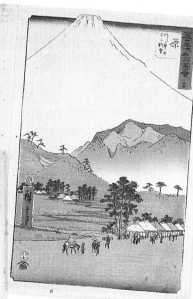

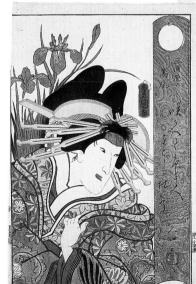

JAPANESE PRINTS
These two prints were modified by van Gogh for the background to Père Tanguy's portrait. *Hara* (above), by Hiroshige, has been given a red sky with bamboos, and the mountain a more detailed form. The *Geisha* (left) by Toyokuni III (Kunisada) has been revised and colored differently. Van Gogh's collection of Japanese prints numbered about 400.

Sunflowers

THESE FIERY BLOOMS have become van Gogh's personal emblem. Few artists had attempted them before, and since then few have dared risk comparison with van Gogh's masterpieces. He started painting sunflowers in Paris, at first mixed with other blooms, but then alone, in paintings of great originality and power. In Arles he painted them simply for the decoration of the Yellow House (p. 44) in honor of Gauguin's arrival, and it is those with yellow backgrounds that are the most stunningly original. These "decorations" triumphantly transcended their modest purpose, and they provide, more successfully than any other of van Gogh's pictures, the universal appeal that was one of his most cherished ideals.

Sunflower
in bloom

Four Sunflowers

1887; 23½ x 39½ in (60 x 100 cm)
This is one of the most remarkable pictures van Gogh painted in Paris or, indeed, anywhere else. On several Paris canvases he conveyed the powerful magnetism that drew him to the south, but nowhere more explicitly than here. The flowers, like flickering flames of kindling, would later become a solid blaze of almost pure yellow and orange (far right).

COLOR SCHEME
Pale yellow is the
dominant hue of the flowers, enlivened by the use of orange. The complementary colors of blue and orange, and red and green, are used consciously, but not too obviously.

SUBTLE COMPOSITION
The variations of color
and brushwork are extremely subtle. The eye is obliged to scan continually the whole picture, while always returning to the three flowers that are showing their faces.

SEED TEXTURE
The seeds can be
compared to an undulating landscape of corn stubble. The tiny brushstrokes were no doubt rapidly applied and they show just how precise and accurate van Gogh could be.

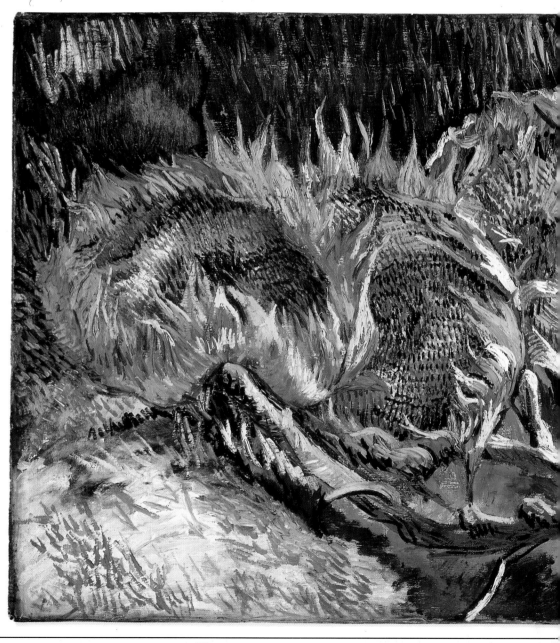

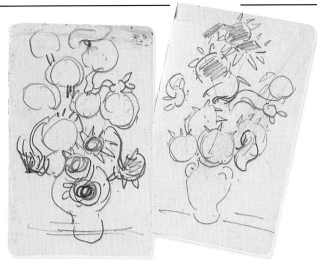

SUNFLOWER SKETCHES
These sketches were almost certainly made at Auvers (p. 58), at least 18 months after the original decorations for the Yellow House. They may have been sketched to describe the pictures to Dr. Gachet, or were perhaps related to a projected series of etchings, *Memories of the South*, which never came to fruition.

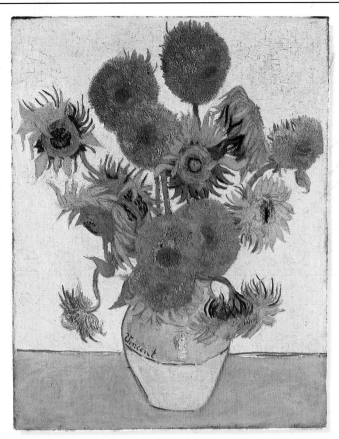

FOURTEEN SUNFLOWERS
1888; 37 x 28¾ in (93 x 73 cm)
In a letter after his breakdown, van Gogh referred to the "high yellow note" he had struck during the summer of 1888, most powerfully exemplified by his series of five almost entirely yellow paintings of sunflowers. It was an astonishing achievement, as proved by the canvas above. In contrast to *Four Sunflowers* (left), van Gogh exploits the basic colors of the sunflower – the yellow entirely dominant. He thus scaled a pinnacle of chromatic intensity.

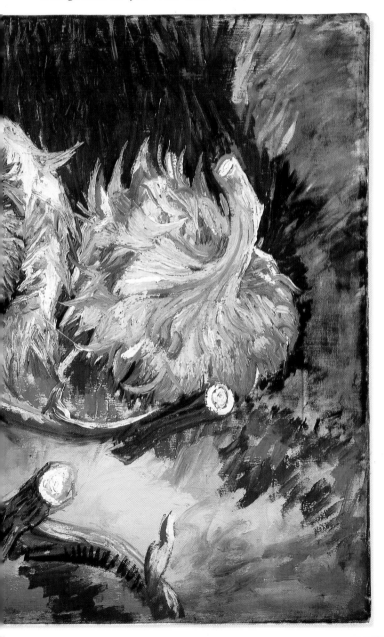

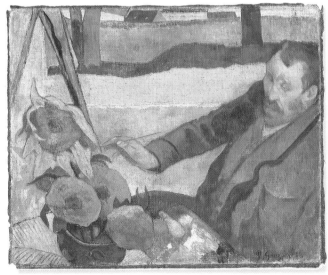

PORTRAIT OF VAN GOGH PAINTING SUNFLOWERS
Paul Gauguin; 1888; 28¾ x 36 in (73 x 91 cm)
Pictures of painters at work are rare, and Gauguin at least partly invented this one, since van Gogh had painted his sunflowers before his hero's arrival – van Gogh's stance and the angles of his canvas do seem unnatural. According to Gauguin, his friend commented, "That's me all right, but me gone mad." But the picture could simply suggest the judicious care with which the sunflowers were painted.

A study in yellow

IN THE AUTUMN of 1887, after painting his extraordinary masterpiece of cut sunflowers and its companions (pp. 38–39), van Gogh began a series of equally astonishing still lifes, mainly of fruit. The artist had spent the first half of the year absorbing Impressionist and pointillist techniques (pp. 34–35) in landscape and self-portraiture; but in painting the still lifes he was clearly looking further into the future. In them he sought to find a powerful synthesis of his draftsman's painting with pure and sometimes quite arbitrary color. The resulting pictures include the extraordinary *Lemons, Pears, Apples, Grapes, and an Orange*, and seem less dependent on close observation of the subject than almost anything he would paint, even at St. Rémy (p. 48). They could be seen as highly charged decoration or, remembering van Gogh's interest in musical equivalents for color, loud introductory fanfares.

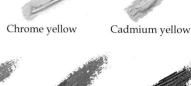

Chrome yellow   Cadmium yellow

Chrome orange   Vermilion   Red ochre

ARTIST'S PALETTE
Van Gogh benefited from developments in the production of new, more stable pigments. Their greater availability encouraged the Impressionists to use brighter and more varied colors. In the canvas below, van Gogh displays this – yellows, ochres, and browns are accented by red, green, blue, and white.

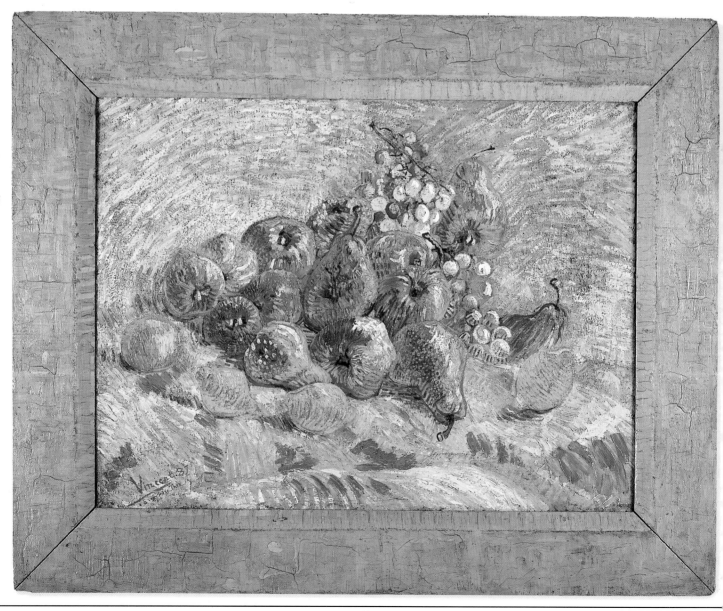

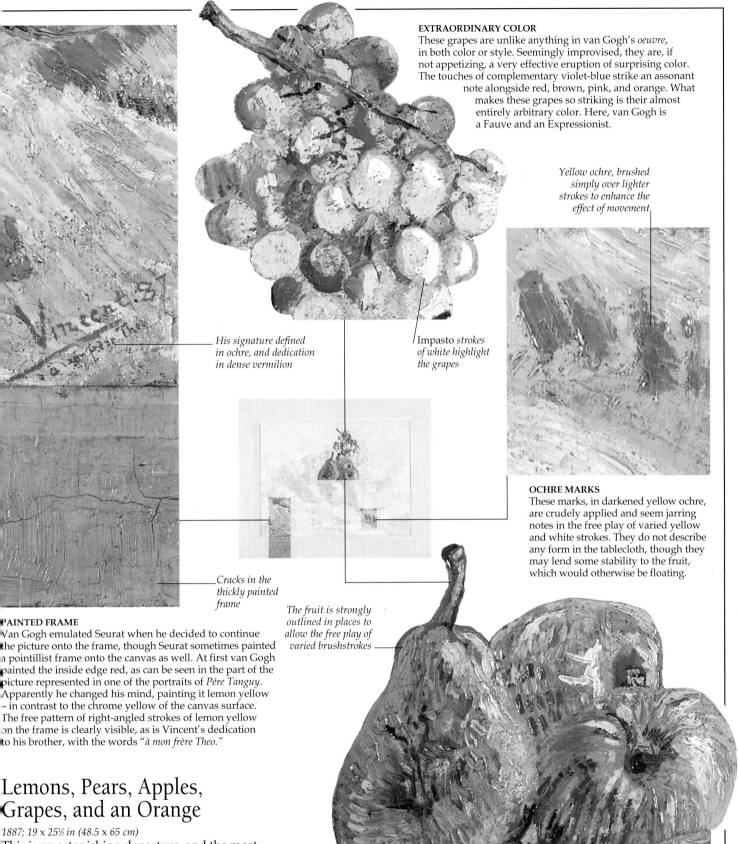

EXTRAORDINARY COLOR

These grapes are unlike anything in van Gogh's *oeuvre*, in both color or style. Seemingly improvised, they are, if not appetizing, a very effective eruption of surprising color. The touches of complementary violet-blue strike an assonant note alongside red, brown, pink, and orange. What makes these grapes so striking is their almost entirely arbitrary color. Here, van Gogh is a Fauve and an Expressionist.

Yellow ochre, brushed simply over lighter strokes to enhance the effect of movement

His signature defined in ochre, and dedication in dense vermilion

Impasto strokes of white highlight the grapes

OCHRE MARKS

These marks, in darkened yellow ochre, are crudely applied and seem jarring notes in the free play of varied yellow and white strokes. They do not describe any form in the tablecloth, though they may lend some stability to the fruit, which would otherwise be floating.

Cracks in the thickly painted frame

The fruit is strongly outlined in places to allow the free play of varied brushstrokes

PAINTED FRAME

Van Gogh emulated Seurat when he decided to continue the picture onto the frame, though Seurat sometimes painted a pointillist frame onto the canvas as well. At first van Gogh painted the inside edge red, as can be seen in the part of the picture represented in one of the portraits of *Père Tanguy*. Apparently he changed his mind, painting it lemon yellow – in contrast to the chrome yellow of the canvas surface. The free pattern of right-angled strokes of lemon yellow on the frame is clearly visible, as is Vincent's dedication to his brother, with the words *"à mon frère Theo."*

Lemons, Pears, Apples, Grapes, and an Orange

1887; 19 x 25½ in (48.5 x 65 cm)

This is an astonishing departure, and the most radical of eight paintings of fruit (and one of books) made around the same time. It is pure color and pure painting. The uninterrupted color relates it to the earlier still lifes of potatoes and birds' nests at Nuenen (pp. 18–19), though here it is yellow that dominates. The tints of the paint are expressive rather than descriptive, and the tablecloth has become virtually abstract – simply a field of turbulent movement.

APPLES AND PEARS

There is very little of what is called *chiaroscuro* (the definition of form through darkness and light) in the picture, except in the recess of the apple core and the yellow highlight strokes that describe the fruits' shape. The red strokes on the pear seem more arbitrary, making the surface appear bruised and seething with sunspots. On the left of the pear, alternate strokes of chrome orange and yellow create a decorative pattern and shape the fruit. The varied brushstrokes are interesting for being more than descriptive. There is little doubt, from what he wrote, that van Gogh could envisage creating an entirely abstract painting.

The lure of the south

VAN GOGH LEFT PARIS for the south of France in February 1888, settling in the Provençal town of Arles. Life in the capital with Theo had become a strain, and van Gogh felt he needed an entirely new territory he could call his own. At first he was filled with hope, feeling that the people of Arles were "more artistic than in the north in their own persons and manner of life." He was excited by the colors of the south and painted the few friends he made. In addition to portraying his landlady, Madame Ginoux, as *L'Arlésienne*, he depicted the café where he lodged, staying up for three nights to paint its interior and some regulars. He hoped *The Night Café* expressed "the powers of darkness in a public house," but as an attempt to portray human degradation, it was, perhaps, a failure.

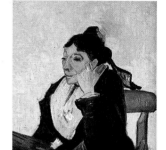

L'ARLESIENNE
1888; 36½ x 29 in (93 x 74 cm)
Impressed by the line and color of traditional Arlésienne costume, van Gogh painted Madame Ginoux, the landlady of *The Night Café*. He painted her after moving out of his lodgings at the café, referring to an earlier drawing of her by Gauguin. Seven versions of the painting exist and they seem icons of a kind – symbolic female figures represented in a sympathetic manner.

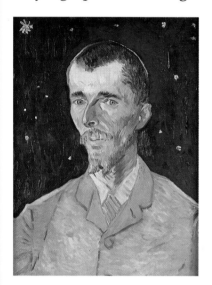

EUGENE BOCH
1888; 23½ x 17¾ in (60 x 45 cm);
Eugène Boch was a Belgian artist who van Gogh met in Arles. Van Gogh wanted to paint a poet "type," and he found Boch physically similar to Dante. This is only a study for a more ambitious project, *Poet against a Starry Sky*, which he painted in Boch's absence, but then destroyed, deciding never to work without a model.

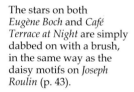

The stars on both *Eugène Boch* and *Café Terrace at Night* are simply dabbed on with a brush, in the same way as the daisy motifs on *Joseph Roulin* (p. 43).

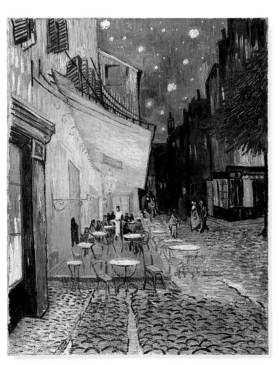

CAFE TERRACE AT NIGHT
1888; 32 x 26 in (81 x 65.5 cm)
This external view of a café on the Place du Forum in Arles was painted shortly after *The Night Café*. In a letter to his sister Wil, he gives an almost rapturous description of the painting: "... here there is a night picture without any black, nothing but beautiful blue and violet and green, and in those surroundings the lighted square is colored sulphur yellow and limey green." He concluded with the words, "I really enjoy doing a painting on the spot at night."

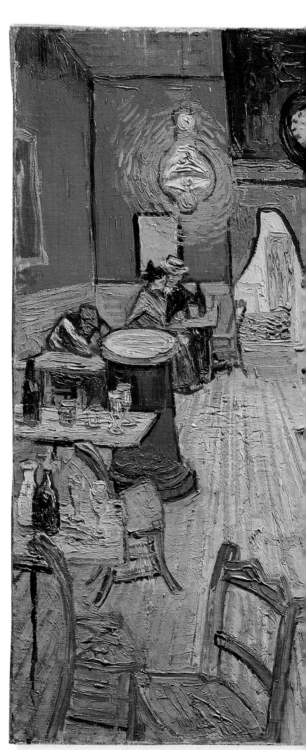

The Night Café

1888; 27½ x 35 in (70 x 89 cm)

Through his unconventional use of color, van Gogh saw *The Night Café* as a statement on the human condition. "It is the equivalent, though different, of *The Potato Eaters* ... I have tried to express the terrible passions of humanity by means of red and green," the artist wrote. For all his intelligence he was sometimes naive. The picture gives no moral shock, and if anything it provokes our concern for the customers' boredom and the Ginoux's slow trade. In fact, the picture could be seen as a rather wonderful failure – an involuntary expression of van Gogh's compassion.

ARLES NEWSPAPER
Van Gogh's relations with the people of Arles turned sour after his self-mutilation (p. 44) – reported in the local newspaper. Local people organized a petition to have him removed from the town, with no doubt exaggerated accounts of his conduct. He was not only grievously ill, but an outcast.

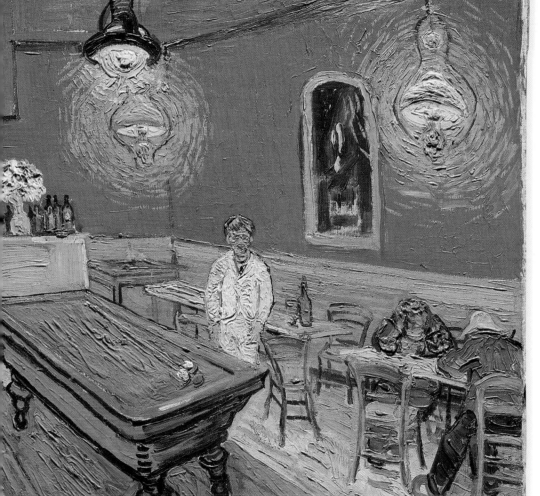

ATMOSPHERIC COLOR
The red of the walls and green of the ceiling are very flat and deliberately dominant. The still life of flowers and the bottles on the bar could almost be an altar, as the artist intended, but not to anything like the "terrible passions of humanity."

THE LAMPS
This style of oil lamp was also seen in *The Potato Eaters* (p. 22). Alternating dabs of orange, green, and yellow against the dark red background create the shimmering effect of the lamps.

THE CAFE SCENE
Only two of the customers, a man and woman in the corner, are awake. Monsieur Ginoux (or the waiter?) seems more concerned with watching the artist than clearing the tables. The atmosphere is one of torpidity rather than visciousness.

DRAWN TO THE KITCHEN
The compelling perspective of the floor pulls the eye through the shadow of the billiard table and through to the kitchen, with its curious drape over the doorway.

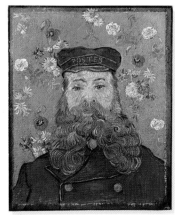

JOSEPH ROULIN
1889; 25¼ x 21½ in (64 x 54.5 cm)
Van Gogh described his best friend in Arles as "… such a good soul, and so wise and so full of feeling and so trustful." Along with the six paintings of Roulin, there are also several of his wife, five of which are titled *La Berceuse* (The Lullaby).

Van Gogh and Gauguin

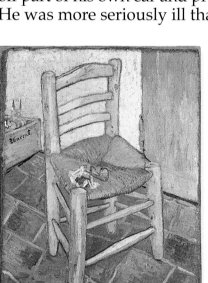

THE YELLOW HOUSE
This photograph shows the house (on the right) that van Gogh rented for himself and Gauguin to live in.

VAN GOGH WANTED ARLES to become a center for artists and, with no little difficulty, persuaded Paul Gauguin to join him in late October 1888. By then Vincent had rented the Yellow House, which he decorated with some of his most joyful works in Gauguin's honor. His hopes for their association were high, but disagreements were not long delayed. Seeing himself as the more enlightened artist, Gauguin could not resist mockery. Van Gogh came to see Gauguin's pressure on him to paint from the imagination (rather than from nature) as an intolerable threat to his work, and his hidden illness erupted in a terrible crisis. On December 23, he cut off part of his own ear and presented it to a local prostitute. He was more seriously ill than anyone had realized.

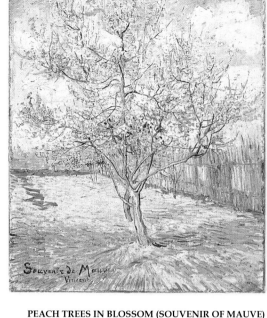

CHAIR WITH PIPE
1888; 35½ x 28½ in (90.5 x 72 cm)
This painting was inspired by *The Empty Chair*, an engraving in *The London Graphic* commemorating Charles Dickens's death (p. 15). Van Gogh painted this and its companion, *Gauguin's Chair*, a few days before his first breakdown and Gauguin's departure from Arles. In them he subtly compares their unfortunately polarized characters.

PEACH TREES IN BLOSSOM (SOUVENIR OF MAUVE)
1888; 28½ x 23½ in (73 x 59.5 cm)
When van Gogh read an obituary of Anton Mauve, his teacher in The Hague (p. 14), he was moved to send a painting to Mauve's widow inscribed with his name and Theo's – the latter was subsequently removed, probably at his brother's request. Another motive in sending it was to impress Hermanus Tersteeg, a dealer who was van Gogh's superior at Goupil's in The Hague, but who had long since washed his hands of him.

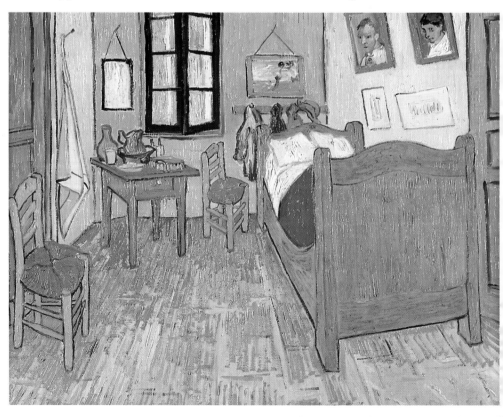

VAN GOGH'S BEDROOM
1889; 22 x 29 in (56.5 x 74 cm)
This painting, among van Gogh's best-known and best-loved images, is one of two copies he made in St. Rémy of the 1888 original painted in Arles. It was first painted to celebrate the achievement of domestic stability at the Yellow House. Theo felt the painting was such a good piece of work that he suggested Vincent make another copy of it. Curiously, George Eliot partly inspired it with her novel *Felix Holt*, the story of a man of means who devotes his life to the poor and adopts a humble way of life. It provides a touching insight into van Gogh's hopes at Arles, and he was very pleased with the picture, regarding it as one of his best: "Virile and simple ... only flat colors in harmony," he wrote. The Yellow House never lost its aura for him.

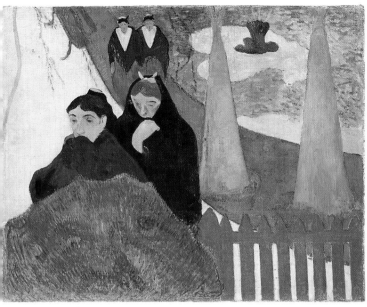

OLD WOMEN AT ARLES
Paul Gauguin; 1888; 29 x 36 in (73 x 92 cm)
This is a companion or rival to van Gogh's "garden" (below). The women, one of them perhaps Madame Ginoux (p. 42), are wrapped up against the mistral wind. Their green faces could provoke sympathy. Van Gogh's painting is certainly the more beautiful one.

FELLOW ARTIST
Paul Gauguin was to become the legendary painter of the South Seas. In 1902, he wrote of van Gogh: "... a man who was cared for in an insane asylum, yet who regained enough of his reason ... to understand his condition, and paint furiously the wonderful pictures people are now so familiar with."

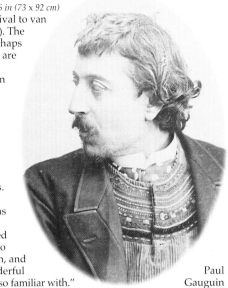

Paul Gauguin

MEMORY OF THE GARDEN AT ETTEN
1888; 29 x 36 in (73.5 x 92.5 cm)
This was painted willingly under the influence of Gauguin: "Gauguin gives me courage to imagine things, and certainly things done from imagination take on a more mysterious character," wrote van Gogh. The picture is intended to evoke the gardens at Etten and Nuenen through the presence of his mother and his sister, Wil. Van Gogh's own "Gauguin" is beautiful even if, as he soon decided, he was taking the wrong turning by following this path.

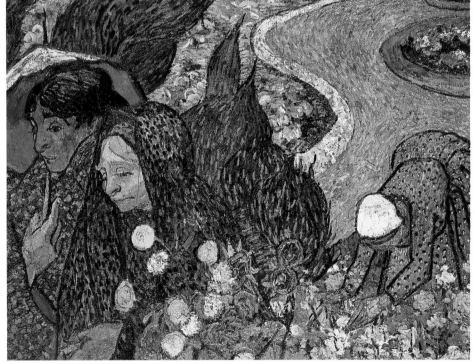

VARIETY OF COLOR
This is a sample box of French pigments of the late 19th century. At Arles, van Gogh employed (as well as lead white and some earth colors) red lake, vermilion, cadmium yellow, ultramarine, cobalt violet, emerald green, and viridian. He painted with the most intense colors, partly in the knowledge that the colors would fade in time as they were not "light fast" (p. 63).

Transactions with the van Goghs

GAUGUIN'S NOTEBOOK
This is a page from a notebook that contained a record of the disposal of Gauguin's paintings. Van Gogh's entry in the book possibly concerns the gift of a painting or drawing from Gauguin to his fellow artist. The other circled entry is a Martinique picture of 1887 that had been sold to Theo van Gogh. It was, in fact, only financial assistance from Theo that induced Gauguin to join Vincent at Arles.

A heroic self-portrait

1889; 23½ x 19¼ in (60 x 49 cm)

Van Gogh painted two self-portraits with his ear bandaged soon after his self-mutilation, and this one is the more subtle and reflective of the two. Painted within two weeks of his breakdown, it is a remarkably dispassionate and entirely dignified self-image. By confronting himself calmly under a strong light, he was asserting that he was alive and well. The image is not simply anecdotal; it suggests a new confidence: "I hope I have just had simply an artist's fit ... serenity returns to my brain day by day," Vincent wrote to Theo.

I**F VAN GOGH HAD NOT RECOVERED** from the terrible breakdown he suffered on December 23, 1888, Theo, Gauguin, and his few good friends would have accepted it as the almost inevitable disintegration of an extraordinary, but sorely afflicted, man. However, he was to suffer further – from a repeated cycle of acute nervous distress and delusions followed by exhaustion and a subsequent period of well-being and lucidity. His condition may yet become explicable in medical terms. The *Self-portrait with Bandaged Ear* is a monument to his resilience after his first attack, and tells of the spirit that would enable him to complete over 450 works before he finally foundered.

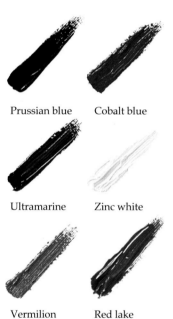

Prussian blue   Cobalt blue

Ultramarine   Zinc white

Vermilion   Red lake

PAINTING MATERIALS
The Courtauld Institute, London, identified the above pigments used in this self-portrait. It is likely that van Gogh also painted with black, chrome yellow, and unidentifiable greens. The painting was lined with lead in France in around 1920, probably for preservation purposes. This has restricted analysis, since X-rays are illegible. There are, however, traces of a charcoal drawing, visible on the bare areas of a relatively coarse-weave canvas. The application of paint is often sparse, perhaps to convey a more neutral atmosphere.

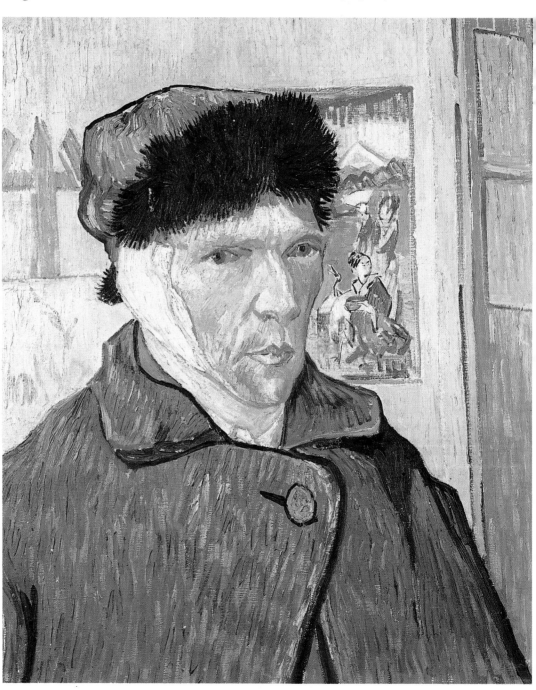

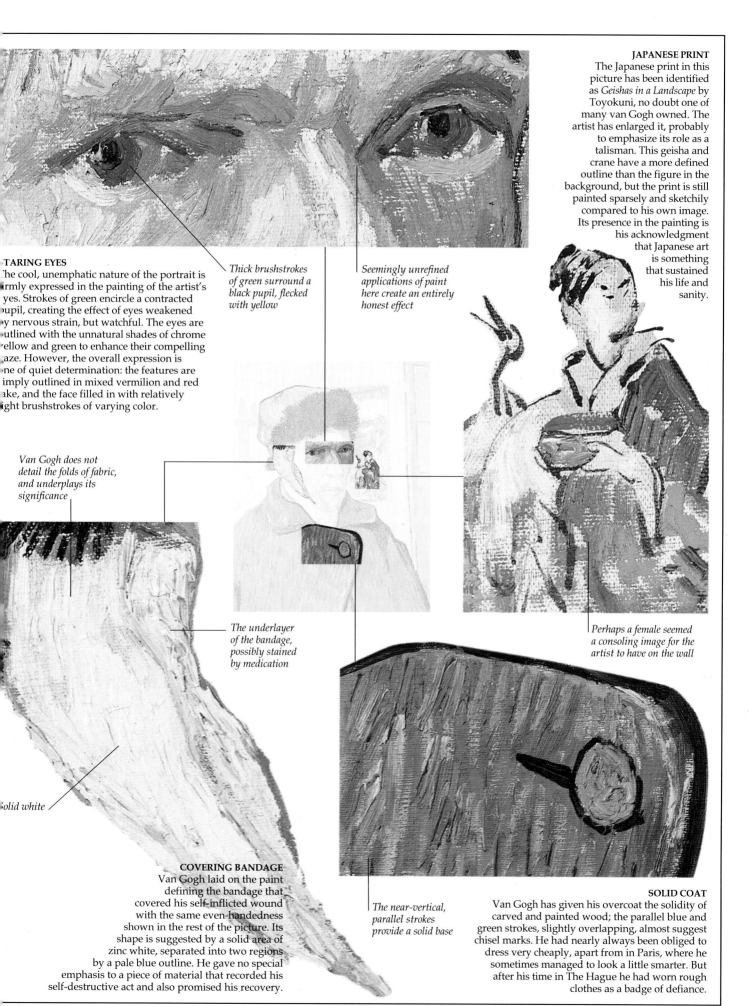

JAPANESE PRINT
The Japanese print in this picture has been identified as *Geishas in a Landscape* by Toyokuni, no doubt one of many van Gogh owned. The artist has enlarged it, probably to emphasize its role as a talisman. This geisha and crane have a more defined outline than the figure in the background, but the print is still painted sparsely and sketchily compared to his own image. Its presence in the painting is his acknowledgment that Japanese art is something that sustained his life and sanity.

STARING EYES
The cool, unemphatic nature of the portrait is firmly expressed in the painting of the artist's eyes. Strokes of green encircle a contracted pupil, creating the effect of eyes weakened by nervous strain, but watchful. The eyes are outlined with the unnatural shades of chrome yellow and green to enhance their compelling gaze. However, the overall expression is one of quiet determination: the features are simply outlined in mixed vermilion and red lake, and the face filled in with relatively light brushstrokes of varying color.

Thick brushstrokes of green surround a black pupil, flecked with yellow

Seemingly unrefined applications of paint here create an entirely honest effect

Van Gogh does not detail the folds of fabric, and underplays its significance

The underlayer of the bandage, possibly stained by medication

Perhaps a female seemed a consoling image for the artist to have on the wall

olid white

COVERING BANDAGE
Van Gogh laid on the paint defining the bandage that covered his self-inflicted wound with the same even-handedness shown in the rest of the picture. Its shape is suggested by a solid area of zinc white, separated into two regions by a pale blue outline. He gave no special emphasis to a piece of material that recorded his self-destructive act and also promised his recovery.

The near-vertical, parallel strokes provide a solid base

SOLID COAT
Van Gogh has given his overcoat the solidity of carved and painted wood; the parallel blue and green strokes, slightly overlapping, almost suggest chisel marks. He had nearly always been obliged to dress very cheaply, apart from in Paris, where he sometimes managed to look a little smarter. But after his time in The Hague he had worn rough clothes as a badge of defiance.

The afflicted artist

DR. REY
Dr. Felix Rey was the sympathetic intern at the Arles hospital whom van Gogh would "immortalize" within three weeks or so of his collapse.

From December 1888 until his death in July 1890, van Gogh was chronically, and often acutely, sick, albeit with brief periods of deceptive well-being. After another crisis at Arles and hospitalization there, he became a voluntary patient in the asylum at St. Rémy in May 1889. Epilepsy was diagnosed; but recent medical opinion suggests that it may have been acute intermittent porphyria. This might explain some puzzling aspects of his case and could account for Theo's final insanity, as the disease is congenital. Whatever it was – and syphilis is also a candidate – it overwhelmed Vincent periodically, causing him appalling distress and delusions of persecution. It is extraordinary how prolific he was during these 19 months, despite being incapacitated for one third of the time.

ARLES HOSPITAL
1889; 29 x 36¼ in (74 x 92 cm)
This is one of two paintings van Gogh made of the hospital at Arles shortly before his departure from the town. Both convey a kind of acceptance of what had happened to him. The interior with its near-complementary harmony of blue and red-brown to orange, is calm. The patients sit, resigned, around the stove in the January chill as the nuns proceed on their charitable rounds. A crucifix emphasizes the vanishing point of the perspective, although it seems entirely incidental. It says something of van Gogh's character that he could contemplate the setting of his intense suffering with such benign and artistic detachment.

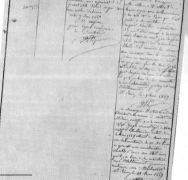
Record of van Gogh's entry into the asylum

ASYLUM ADVERTISEMENT
In its prospectus of the time, the asylum at St. Rémy de Provence expressed quiet pride in its location, its buildings, its facilities for worship, its enlightened treatment of the mentally ill – and even its food. There were four classes of patient, the top one of "higher boarders" having apartments "with luxury," and the possibility of a servant. Van Gogh was in the third class at 800 francs a year – all Theo could afford on top of his provision of paints and canvas for his brother. It paid for a bedroom and a room for a studio.

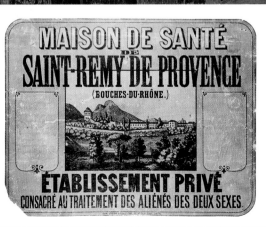
MAISON DE SANTÉ
DE
SAINT-REMY DE PROVENCE
(BOUCHES-DU-RHÔNE.)
ÉTABLISSEMENT PRIVÉ
CONSACRÉ AU TRAITEMENT DES ALIÉNÉS DES DEUX SEXES.

THE DIAGNOSIS
Dr. Peyron's description of van Gogh's condition in the register of the asylum mentions hallucinations of sight and hearing and "lack of strength and courage to live in freedom." He diagnoses epilepsy and states the necessity for prolonged observation.

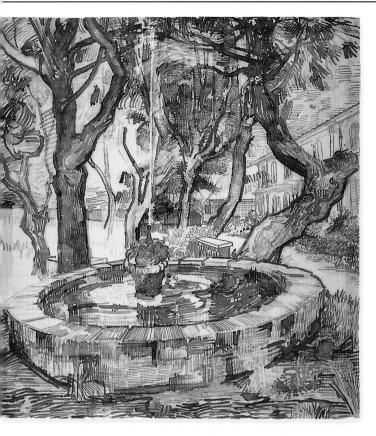

FOUNTAIN IN THE GARDEN OF THE ASYLUM

At St. Rémy, van Gogh soon took up the reed and steel pens with which he had made such beautiful drawings around Arles. He sent the new ones to Theo – who had been very enthusiastic about this kind of drawing – to show him what kind of subject matter he was now involved with. This exciting delineation of the garden fountain has magnificent vigor and accuracy, and the geometry of the basin has been mastered effortlessly. Van Gogh now had all the perspective frame he needed in his head – and the Provençal cypress tree was a subject awaiting his virtuosity with the pen (pp. 54–55).

VAN GOGH'S CONFINEMENT

Even though van Gogh was committed to the asylum (right) because of his mental illness, he was actually only "mad" when in the grip of an attack, and his recoveries always seemed complete. Because of this, he was sympathetically treated, and restrictions on his movements were relaxed after about a month. In July, he suffered another attack and was confined indoors. He was incapable of work for about six weeks, although on resuming he painted more than 18 pictures in 26 days.

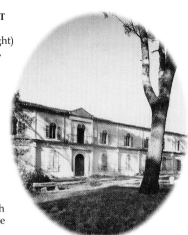

SAINT-PAUL HOSPITAL

1889; 25 x 18 in (63 x 48 cm)
When painting close to the asylum, (also known as Saint-Paul Hospital), van Gogh would rarely emphasize the building itself, though he made at least three gouaches of the interior. The figures of patients that sometimes appear do not convey Vincent's difficult relations with them. He described them to Theo with a sympathy tinged with black humor, but he undoubtedly often found them disturbing. He actually ascribed his last crushing attack to "the influence of the other patients."

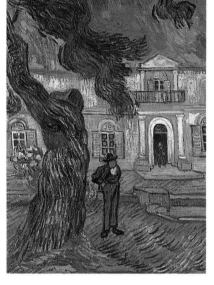

SELF-PORTRAIT

1889; 25½ x 21¼ in (65 x 54 cm)
On recovering from his first six-week breakdown at St. Rémy, which struck in mid-July 1889, van Gogh kept himself confined to his studio for a time and painted two very powerful portraits. The first was possibly intended to persuade the hospital authorities not to prevent him working. This, the second one, seems like a ruthless self-examination and a declaration of unshakeable resolve.

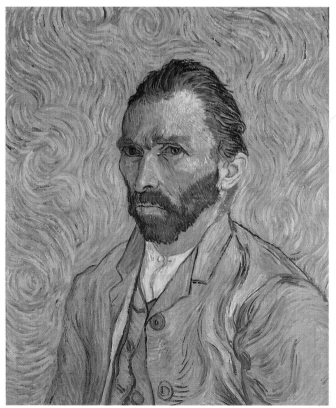

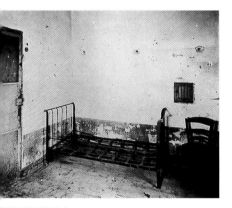

THE BEDROOM

"Van Gogh's bedroom in the asylum had greenish gray wallpaper and curtains of sea green ... very pretty in design."

THE BATHROOM

Baths were a regular part of the asylum's regimen of treatment. "I have a bath twice a week now and stay in it for two hours," wrote van Gogh.

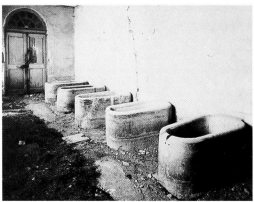

Natural studies

A<small>T</small> S<small>T</small>. R<small>ÉMY</small>, the garden of the asylum very soon compelled van Gogh to make color sing as never before. During the first two weeks, he painted two masterpieces, one of lilacs and one of irises – a flower first featured at Arles, but here made the dominant subject. It is easy to understand their attraction for him, with their vivid violet-blue together with their complex and seemingly animated forms. As a motif they are almost as arresting as sunflowers, as positive and even more overtly dynamic. Van Gogh painted the iris as a positively thrilling flower.

Irises

A cicada, with wings open

CICADAS
These sketches of cicadas were sent in a letter to Theo. "Their song ... has the same charm for me as the cricket on the hearth for the peasants at home," wrote van Gogh.

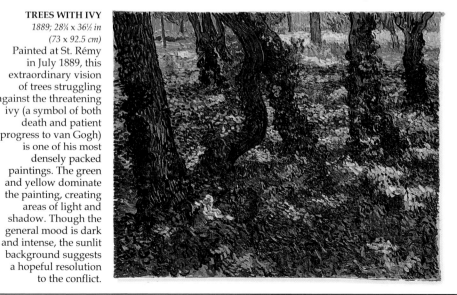

TREES WITH IVY
1889; 28¾ x 36½ in (73 x 92.5 cm)
Painted at St. Rémy in July 1889, this extraordinary vision of trees struggling against the threatening ivy (a symbol of both death and patient progress to van Gogh) is one of his most densely packed paintings. The green and yellow dominate the painting, creating areas of light and shadow. Though the general mood is dark and intense, the sunlit background suggests a hopeful resolution to the conflict.

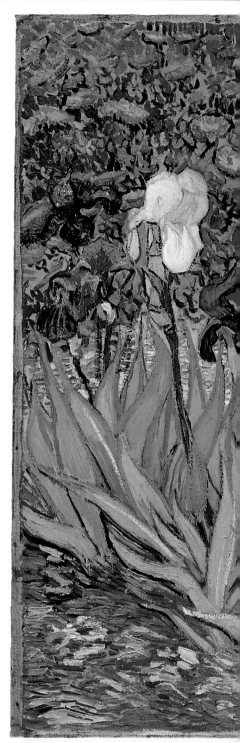

Irises

1889; 28 x 36½ in (71 x 93 cm)
This celebrated picture expresses the reli van Gogh felt in reaching the safety of the asylum after his hounding by the people of Arles (p. 43). Painted in the asylum garden soon after his arrival, it could seem like an animated crowd at a public celebration, with the marigolds witnessing a procession of the irises. The color is controlled with a sure instinct, an van Gogh's intense feeling does not impa the sense of real flowers, acutely observed

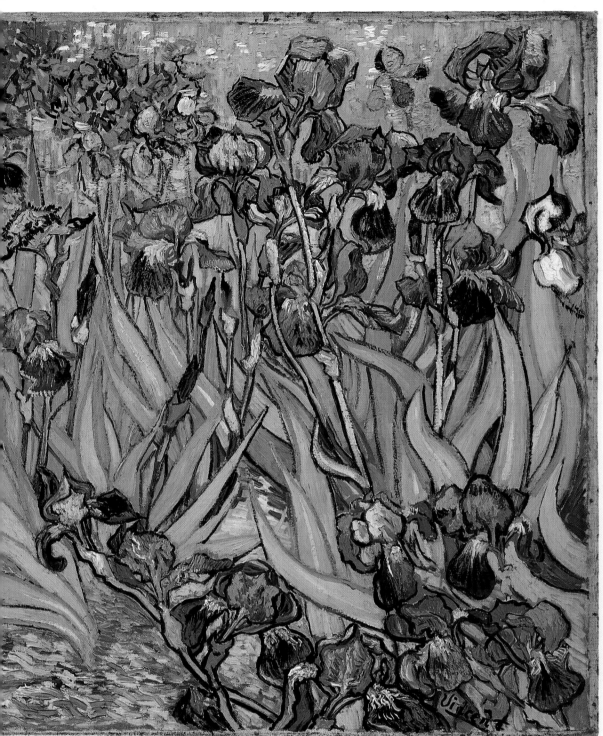

SOFT BACKGROUND
The background is relatively unassertive. On the right, soft white and yellow touches suggest flowers on a rough lawn. On the left, the marigolds glow gently, allowing the complementary violet of the irises full power.

A SWEEP OF IRISES
The iris blooms descend gradually from the top right of the canvas and are thrust forward at the bottom right. They are nearly completely outlined, as if drawn. The flowers seem to be blowing around in a stiff breeze.

DISTINCTIVE LEAVES
The iris leaves are an unusually emphatic turquoise and have points with a more simple upward thrust than the blooms. A surprise note is provided by the large white iris, an outsider among the purple blooms and marigolds.

WARM SOIL
The soil is of a pleasing warm hue and provides a stable base for the riotous dance of the flowers. The paint is brushed on more smoothly, and has a complementary color relationship with the iris leaves.

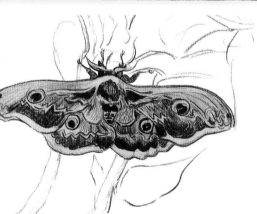

THE MOTH
In May, van Gogh regretfully killed a moth in order to paint it. He waxed lyrical about its coloring, describing it in detail, and sketching "the poor beastie" in a letter. This drawing, in black crayon, pen, and brown ink, indicates van Gogh's abiding interest in details of nature – one that he would show until the last month of his life.

A Great Peacock Moth, as sketched by van Gogh (left)

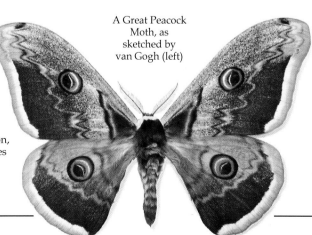

Copies

VAN GOGH ENDURED a number of breakdowns at St. Rémy that entailed acute suffering – two of them following journeys to Arles to visit Madame Ginoux (p. 42). When recovering from the first of these in the asylum, he painted several farm-work scenes, mostly concerning the wheat harvest. He painted copies of etchings made by Millet, and then a painting after a print of a *Pietà* (an image of the dead Christ supported by the Virgin Mary) by Delacroix. He would also work from Doré and Daumier. As well as being works of high quality, all are testimonies of his enduring love of these artists, especially Millet and Delacroix. Copying his favorite painters must have had real therapeutic value, providing a welcome relief before he resumed his more tense personal struggle with painting.

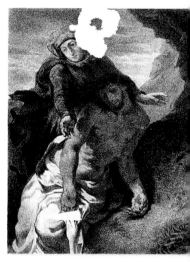

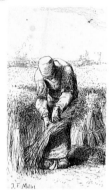

PEASANT WOMAN BINDING SHEAVES
1889; 17 x 13 in (43 x 33 cm)
This is one of eight vignettes of peasants at work, painted after Millet; they are all predominantly yellow and blue with dark outlines. Along with *Peasant Woman Binding Sheaves*, there are two reapers, another sheaf binder, a woman cutting straw, another with a rake, two sheep shearers, and a woman spinning yarn. They are all lighter and somehow more robust than any Millet peasants, and are also testimony to the "work ethic" that van Gogh never lost. He once suggested that painters should work as long and regular hours as ordinary working people.

MILLET'S ORIGINAL
Van Gogh copied prints such as *Peasant Woman Binding Sheaves* (left) as exercises and for pleasure.

PRINT OF PIETÀ
Although van Gogh was often intensely hostile to religion at St. Rémy, he once admitted to Theo that "... religious thoughts sometimes give me great consolation," and he copied from this print by Céléstin Nanteuil of a Delacroix *Pietà*. The romantic image was reversed in the print, and van Gogh's coloring lent it a more acute pathos.

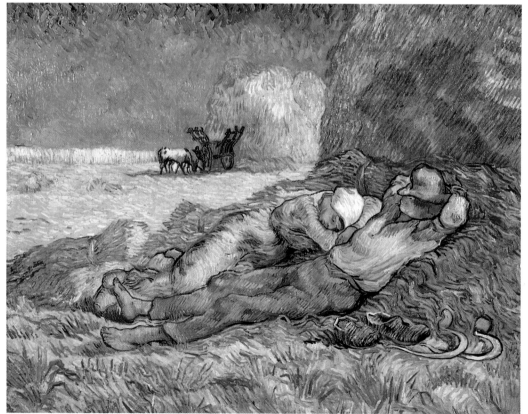

NOON: REST (AFTER MILLET)
1890; 28¾ x 36 in (73 x 91 cm)
This serene image is one of five larger pictures that van Gogh painted after Millet. The heat of the day is entirely unoppressive, with the couple resting in a shade created by their joint labor. The man has discarded his boots (van Gogh's symbols of earnest progress through life), and the sickles lie close together, reflecting the easy intimacy of the figures. Only the ox and cart, as in the original, seem unconvincing. Van Gogh's multidirectional brushstrokes, often used to suggest turbulence or to produce a halo effect, are brilliantly varied to express freedom from tension. The loose brushwork of the foreground stubble enhances the serenity of this lyrical masterpiece.

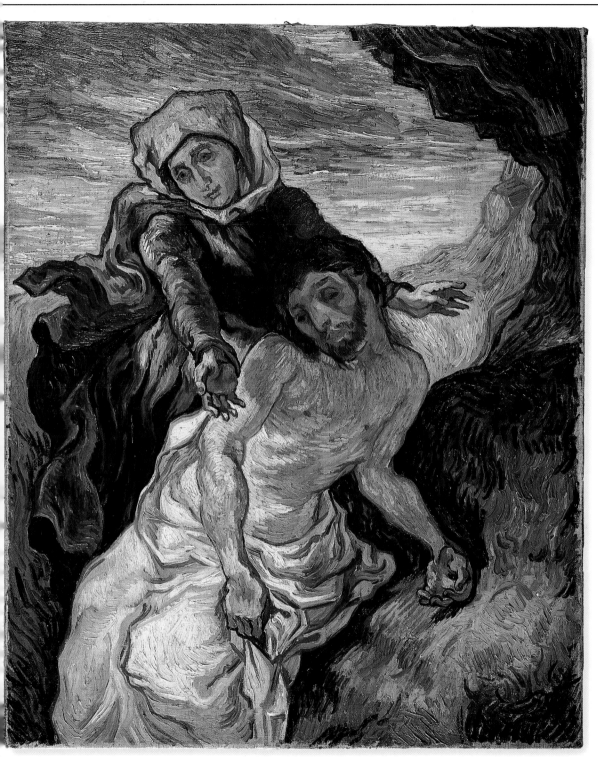

CHRIST OR VINCENT?
It has been suggested that Christ's face is an attempted self-portrait. The hair and beard are a reddish-brown, like van Gogh's, but the similarity of the face to the print after Delacroix (left) discounts this notion.

EXPRESSIVE HANDS
Van Gogh had difficulty painting hands in this picture – "... and yet there are those four hands and arms in the foreground in it – gestures and postures not exactly easy or simple." Although they are a little clumsy, they poignantly express the resigned or appealing helplessness of each figure.

ROLE OF COLOR
The color is gentle, melancholy, and even sickly, but the Virgin's role as a figure of strength is emphasized by the more solid color of her robe. The complementary purple-blue and yellow dominate, though there is a flush of pink to partner the green in the flesh tones.

Pietà (after Delacroix)

1889; 28¾ x 23¾ in (73 x 60.5 cm)

Taken from a monochrome print of the picture, van Gogh painted this while feeling hostile to religion, yet admitting that it could occasionally console him. He felt confident while making his "improvisation" or "translation" – "... if you could see me working, my brain so clear and my fingers so sure that I have drawn that *Pietà* by Delacroix without taking a single measurement." He gave the figures a sickly green flesh, and its melancholy is curiously affecting, as in the original. Van Gogh also made a smaller copy of this painting for his sister, Wil, as well as a copy of another Delacroix picture, *The Good Samaritan*.

LAVIEILLE CARDS
These wood engravings by Jacques-Adrien Lavieille are from Millet's *Labors of the Field*. Van Gogh would probably never have considered making copies from real paintings. The engravings, however, were second-hand versions. They gave him a positive stimulus to attempt evoking the originals, while feeling free to paint them in his own very different way.

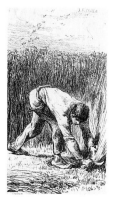

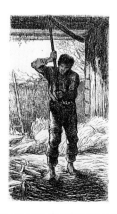

Provençal landscape

AT ST. RÉMY VAN GOGH MADE many forays into the landscape that he had first observed through the bars of his cell. The results were considerably more animated than most of his Arles canvases, and this worried Theo: "How your brain must have labored and how you have pushed everything to the limit, where vertigo is inevitable." *A Cornfield with Cypresses* seems, if just short of this limit, very close to it. Vincent painted at least seven pictures in which the cypress was a dominant subject. He told Theo the trees were "as beautiful … as an Egyptian obelisk … a splash of black in a sunny landscape." In Provence, cypresses were symbols of death, but it seems van Gogh regarded them rather as pillars of strength in the unruliness of the landscape.

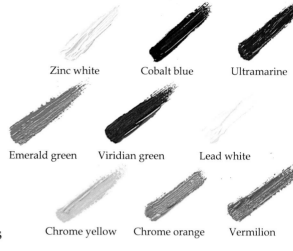

Zinc white   Cobalt blue   Ultramarine

Emerald green   Viridian green   Lead white

Chrome yellow   Chrome orange   Vermilion

ARTIST'S PALETTE
Van Gogh used a range of at least nine paints (above) for this painting. The canvas was prestretched and primed with a traditional oil and lead-white ground. The analysis of the painting, made by the National Gallery, London, found traces of a black pigment, indicating that he drew on the canvas before painting.

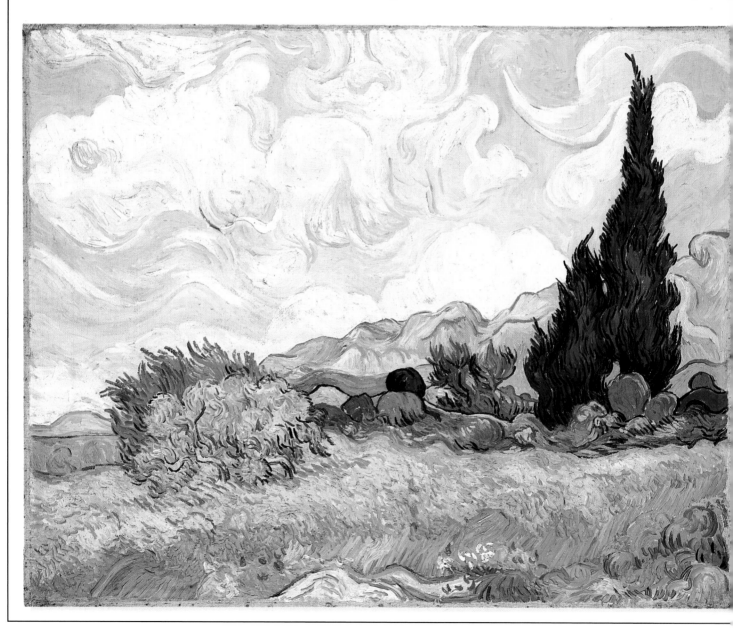

DOMINANT SKY
Van Gogh's thickest *impasto* here tells us that clouds can be as solid as mountains. The sky seems distant, but the cloud formations imply, as they do in *The Roofs of Paris* (pp. 30–31), that the heavens can dominate the most arresting earthly scene. The graphic brushstrokes convey a sense of swirling movement.

Top of cypress painted like the flame of a candle

Contrasting brushstrokes of viridian, emerald green, and ultramarine

Pure cobalt blue

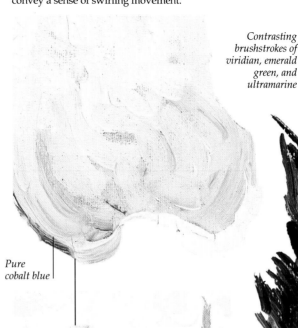

THE CYPRESS
The dark flame of the cypress asserts itself (in dark blue, not black, pigment) as being much stronger than the sky, mountain, or land. No real cypress has such a fiery character or such pointed extremities. To achieve his "black note," van Gogh has brushed light colors onto dark ones. Along with the olive, cypresses were van Gogh's favorite tree at St. Rémy, and he made one the dominant form in this painting.

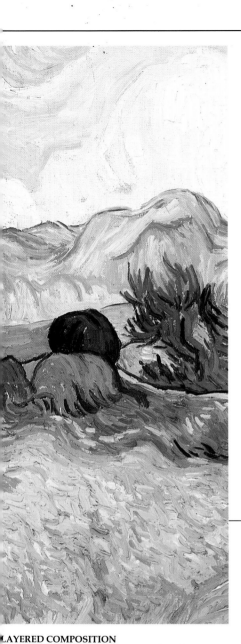

LAYERED COMPOSITION
Vertically and in depth, there are three layers in this composition. Perspective goes hand in hand with color. The foreground is pushed forward by the yellow, and the blues in the background naturally recede. The green middle distance lies comfortably in-between, and there the green-black of the shrub and cypress are deliberately assertive accents between the smooth transition of planes.

Deep ridges of impasto

Pure vermilion poppies

A Cornfield with Cypresses
1889; 28½ x 36 in (72.5 cm x 90.5 cm)
This has, understandably, been one of van Gogh's most reproduced paintings. Painted in September 1889, it is the last in a series of cypress landscapes he finished that year. It expresses his most passionate feelings toward the Provençal countryside. There is a harmony between the different, but related, rhythms created by the artist's delineation of corn, landscape, and sky. The animation of nature is almost alarming, but it is reined in just sufficiently to give the viewer a sense of wonder and excitement.

SEA OF GOLD
In this part of the field, the heavy ears of corn are being pushed down by the stiff breeze, and the brushstrokes curl as they express the corn's struggle to keep standing. The seething mass is described with hundreds of strokes of varying yellows (ochre, sienna, and white), with the random blurring and mixing helping the effect. The field is like a rolling sea of gold or a lion's mane – a triumph of van Gogh's multidirectional brushwork.

An erratic recovery

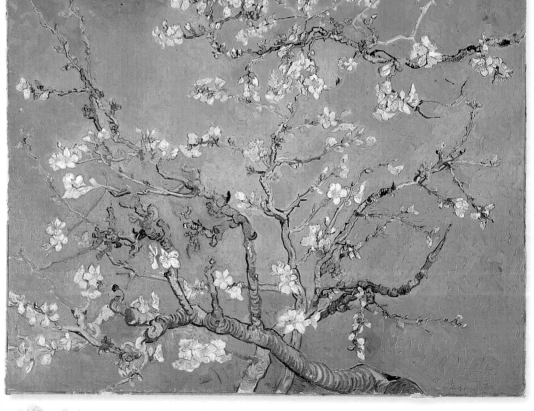

V AN GOGH BEGAN 1890 with a period of recovery and of incident. At the end of January he received the news, which moved him deeply, of the birth of Theo's son, whom the parents named after him. He had also just heard of the publication of the first substantial assessment of his work – an extravagant hymn of praise by the Parisian critic Albert Aurier. But in March he suffered his worst-ever crisis, which prostrated him for nearly two months. On recovering, he insisted on leaving the asylum, and the prospect of liberty inspired one of his greatest creative bursts. Before his departure he finished at least 11 paintings in 16 days, many of them great works. He then set out for Paris to visit Theo and his wife Jo, before moving on to Auvers-sur-Oise (p. 58), an hour from the capital, where he hoped to find a calmer atmosphere for work. Arriving in Paris, he amazed Jo with his robust, cheerful appearance.

RECORD OF LEAVING THE ASYLUM
In the register, Dr. Peyron described the painful details of van Gogh's crises, but added, "In between the attacks, the patient is completely calm and lucid; he then abandons himself with passion to painting." Van Gogh left the asylum for Paris on May 16, 1890.

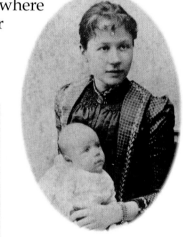

JOHANNA BONGER
Jo Bonger van Gogh, Theo's wife, is the great heroine of Vincent's saga. She never resented his dependence on Theo, and after both their heartbreaking deaths she guarded the flame. Having translated and edited hundreds of his letters, she refused to publish them until his greatness had been established.

BRANCHES OF AN ALMOND TREE IN BLOSSOM
1890; 29 x 36¼ in (73.5 x 92 cm)
This picture was painted to celebrate the birth of Theo and Jo's son. Vincent was as pleased with becoming an uncle as his acutely unhappy circumstances would allow, although nothing could fully allay the "grief" he wrote of several times from the asylum. He would not see the child until he arrived in Paris from St. Rémy, where Vincent contemplated the baby with Theo, tears in their eyes. The design of these almond tree branches is suggestive of "Japonaiserie" kitsch, but in so narrowly avoiding such a quality by subtle drawing and gentle singing color, the work seems doubly moving.

Almond blossom

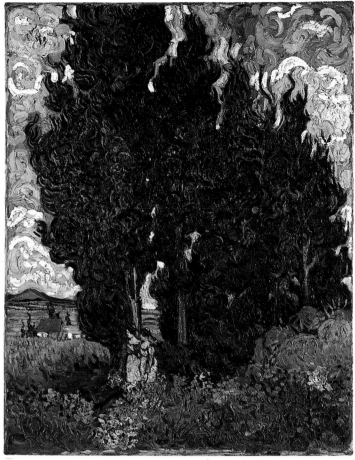

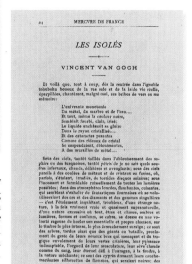

CYPRESSES LETTER
In this letter to Albert Aurier, van Gogh expressed his pleasure at the review, but went on to praise Adolphe Monticelli and Paul Gauguin at his own expense. He promised to send Aurier the cypresses reproduced here, and said he would add one figure to the painting. He actually added two.

AURIER'S REVIEW
Albert Aurier's famous outpouring of almost unqualified praise for van Gogh appeared in the *Mercure de France* in January 1890. It troubled van Gogh at least as much as a courageous homage to him by J.J. Isaacson in the previous August.

CYPRESSES WITH TWO FIGURES
1890; 36¼ x 28¾ in (92 x 73 cm)
This is one of van Gogh's most heavily encrusted paintings, and he seems to have enjoyed applying the dry, solid *impasto*. As in another picture and two other drawings of cypresses, there is a recklessly impassioned feeling to this painting that exceeds that in almost any other work, and certainly surpasses the *Cornfield with Cypresses* (pp. 54–55), started a little later.

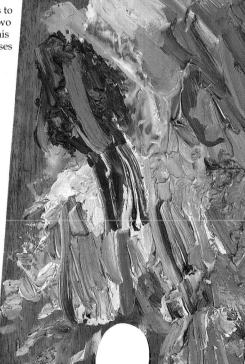

VAN GOGH'S PALETTE
Few palettes remain tidy throughout a picture's execution, and their appearance is not necessarily indicative of a painter's style. But this one, attributed to van Gogh, seems expressive of his perpetual urgency as an artist, though it is possibly the result of only one canvas.

Dabs of paint cleaned from van Gogh's brush

Area near thumb hole free of paint

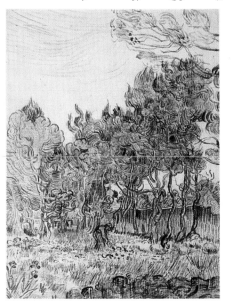

PINE TREES NEAR WALL OF THE ASYLUM
Trees became increasingly fundamental to van Gogh's vision of landscape at St. Rémy. Their animation may express his sense of confinement, as they sometimes seem to be trying to uproot themselves, and their deliberate rhythmic undulation distinguishes them from all others in both drawing and painting.

A return to the north

VAN GOGH ARRIVED AT AUVERS on May 21, 1890. There he received care and friendship from Dr. Paul Gachet, a medical man who was also a patron of artists. The artist's days were outwardly ordered and peaceful, given to work, writing, and sleep. In his letters, there is a willingness to keep going, but with dark notes of foreboding. His wish for his little nephew – "I should like him to have a soul less unquiet than mine, which is foundering ..." – is poignant indeed. He completed almost one painting a day, but they are an uneasy mixture, some undisputed masterpieces, others somewhat forced – and he made some drawings that seem strangely haunted.

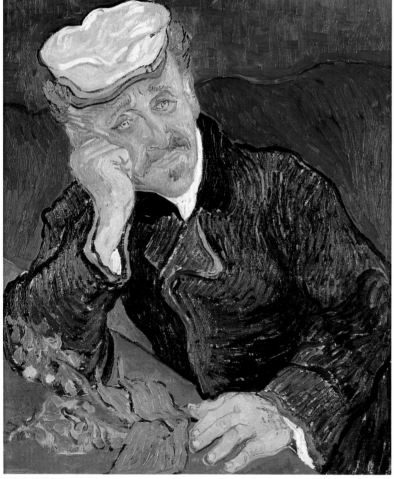

DR. PAUL GACHET
1890; 26¾ x 22½ in (68 x 57 cm)
Paul Gachet was a friend and patron of Paul Cézanne and many other artists. It was Camille Pissarro who roused the doctor's sympathy for van Gogh. The doctor was an unconventional practitioner and high strung; ironically, he provoked van Gogh to speculate as to which of them needed help most. The artist's portraits of the doctor are among his finest, and they express a concerned tenderness for a good man who, however brilliant, could probably not have sustained van Gogh's life for very much longer.

VAN GOGH'S LAST HOME
This is a photograph of what was to be van Gogh's last home – the Ravoux Inn at Auvers, one of the cheapest available.

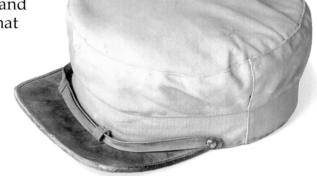

DR. GACHET'S CAP
This is the actual cap worn by Dr. Gachet, and painted by van Gogh in his portrait (left). The artist has accurately rendered elements of the real cap – the brown brim, yellow fastening, and pale color – but enlivened it with his vigorous brushstrokes.

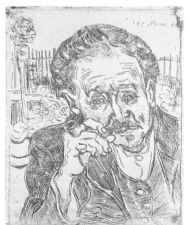

GACHET ETCHING
Dr. Gachet owned an etching press, and this encouraged van Gogh to etch his portrait after painting it. There may be a note of friendly mockery toward the doctor, but it is a totally successful first attempt – "A drawing on metal. I like that drawing very much" – was Theo's verdict.

Foxglove
(*Digitalis purpurea*)

MEDICINAL PLANT
On the table, in the painting of Dr. Gachet, are some foxgloves. The flowers, from which the drug *digitalis* is derived, represent the doctor's profession.

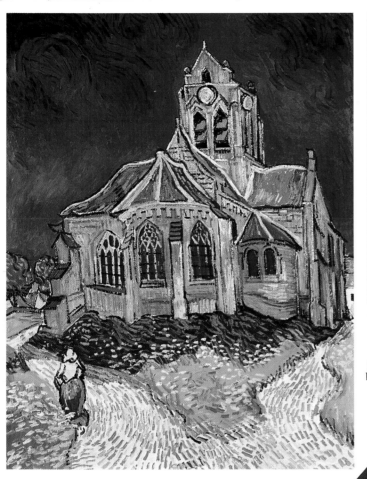

CHURCH AT AUVERS
1890; 37 x 29 in (94 x 74 cm)
One of the best-known images of the Auvers period, this
picture conveys a strong, but enigmatic, emotional charge. Van
Gogh must have found it difficult to contemplate any church
without complex feelings, and he associated this painting with
his ones of the abandoned church tower at Nuenen. He wrote to
his sister, Wil, that in comparison, "the color is more expressive,
more sumptuous" – it could hardly be more so. The thunderous
blue-black sky offers more than a hint of foreboding.

COTTAGES WITH THATCHED ROOFS AT CORDEVILLE
1890; 28 x 36 in (72 x 91 cm)
"Auvers is very beautiful, among other things a lot of old thatched roofs,
which are getting rare," van Gogh wrote in his first letter from there. He
felt nostalgia for thatched cottages while at St. Rémy, and he immediately
began to paint some. The buildings seem fitfully animated, and do not quite
convey the sentiments he had felt toward humble dwellings in Holland.

Drawer for pens

WRITING DESK
This is the writing desk van Gogh
left behind, where he wrote some
of his vast correspondence to Theo;
more than 750 letters survive.

Van Gogh's last and unfinished letter

LAST LETTER
Van Gogh's last letter to Theo was found
in his pocket after his death. It conveys
an acute anxiety about the future. Theo
had given his employers an ultimatum,
threatening to set up a business on his
own – a very risky enterprise. He also
refers to worries about friction between
Theo and Jo. The letter expresses his
appreciation of Theo's steadfast support
– "you have your part in the production
of some canvases, which will retain their
calm even in the catastrophe." Finally,
van Gogh turns to his own sense of
disintegration, writing: "Well, my own
work, I am risking my life for it and
half my reason has gone." It is a tragic
ending to one of the greatest series
of letters ever written.

The final act

STRETCHED TO THE VERY LIMIT, and unable to bear his oppressive burdens any longer, van Gogh killed himself. After completing 70 canvases in as many days at Auvers, he borrowed a revolver, went out into the fields, and shot himself in the stomach. The suicide attempt was, at first, unsuccessful. He lay dying for two days, puffing on his pipe and insisting he had no wish to be saved. He died on July 29, 1890, having so bravely contended with disease, isolation, and his own excessively sensitive, ardent nature. But the energy that for him was exhausted at Auvers is, happily, available to us – in hundreds of radiant canvases and extraordinary drawings.

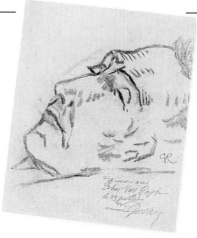

VAN GOGH ON HIS DEATHBED
A gaunt and exhausted van Gogh, drawn by his eccentric guardian Dr. Gachet. The doctor was devoted to van Gogh and his work.

Wheatfield with crows

1890; 20 x 39½ in (50.5 x 100.5 cm)
This canvas has given rise to much speculation and myth-making. It is probably not, as is usually presumed, van Gogh's last picture, and the crows are possibly not flying toward the painter. It is easier to see it as painful and disturbed, rather than expressing the "restorative forces" he mentioned to Theo, concerning his last landscapes. It seems more like exhilaration cruelly turned into despair, and it is no wonder that it has come to be regarded as a tragic and involuntary full stop to his work.

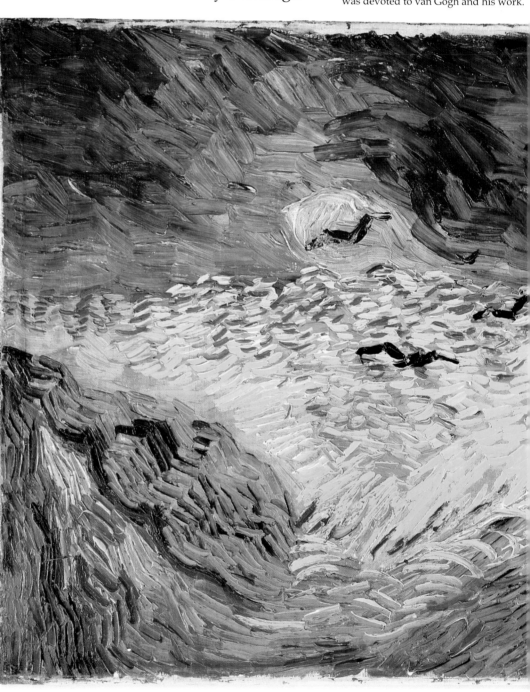

A TURBULENT SCENE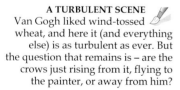
Van Gogh liked wind-tossed wheat, and here it (and everything else) is as turbulent as ever. But the question that remains is – are the crows just rising from it, flying to the painter, or away from him?

DYNAMIC PATHS
This is not the first time van Gogh has used the device of paths leaving the picture on both sides to underscore a central subject. Here their urgent sense of movement is phenomenal, and we will never be sure if the middle path ever escapes the wheatfield.

ANNOUNCEMENT CARD OF VINCENT'S DEATH
Van Gogh died at the age of 37 and, although it was Theo
who organized the formalities after his death, it would
not be long before he himself would share his grave.

VINCENT AND THEO
Six months after Vincent's death,
Theo died. His elder brother's
suicide had shattered him and
he was also extremely ill. At
the hospital in Utrecht,
general paralysis of the
insane – only associated
with syphilis – had been
diagnosed, but he may
also have had the acute
intermittent porphyria,
which was perhaps
Vincent's primary
complaint. Theo suffered
similar delusions of
persecution, and had even
physically attacked Joanna.
But he had truly been Vincent's
indispensable partner, and his
remarkable widow became almost
as important to his brother's future fame.

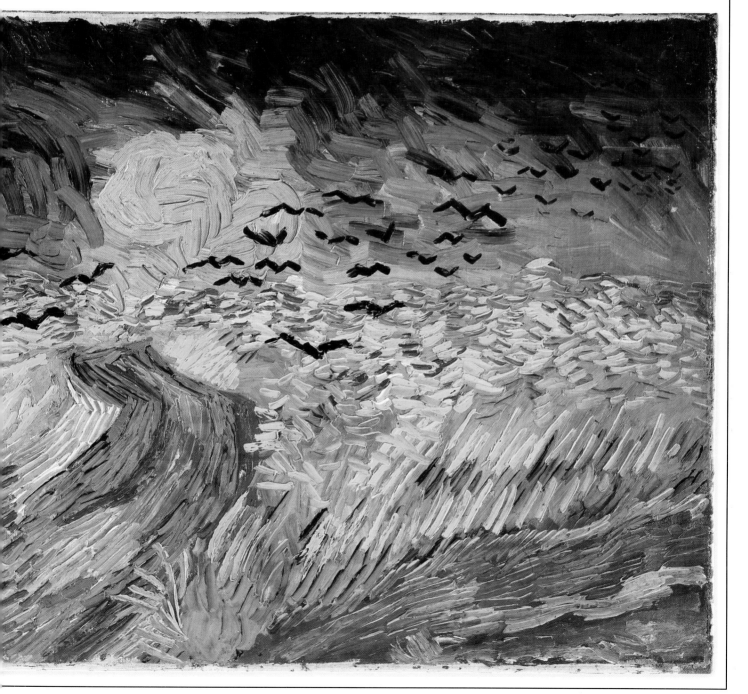

Key biographical dates

1853 Vincent Willem van Gogh born in Groot Zundert, Holland, March 30. Father Theodorus is a pastor, mother is Anna Cornelia Carbentus.

1857 Brother Theo born, May 1.

1869 Leaves school at 15; starts work as a clerk at Goupil & Co., art dealers, in The Hague. Begins correspondence with Theo.

1873 Transfers to Goupil's, London; lives with the Loyers in Hackford Road, Brixton.

1874 Rejection by Eugenie Loyer. Temporary transferral to Paris.

1876 Dismissed April 1; goes to England. Teacher and preacher in Ramsgate, and, from July, preaches in Isleworth. To Etten for Christmas; does not return to England.

1877 Works in a bookshop in Dordrecht. Begins studies at the Theological Seminary in Amsterdam.

1878 Abandons studies in Amsterdam; fails a three-month evangelist course in Brussels.

1878–80 Works as an evangelist lay preacher in the Borinage, a coal-mining district of Belgium. Gives all his possessions away to poor miners' families. Interest in religion wanes, while interest in drawing grows stronger.

1880 Moves to Brussels; decides to become an artist. Theo begins to send Vincent a monthly allowance.

1881 Returns to Etten in April to work and to live with his parents. Falls in love with his cousin, Kee Vos (née Stricker). At Christmas, Vincent argues with father; subsequently leaves for The Hague.

1882 Relationship with Christine Hoornik (Sien), a former prostitute. Begins painting in oils.

1883 Leaves Sien in September. Moves to Drenthe, northern Holland, where he paints and draws harsh life of peasants, but returns three months later to parents' new home at Nuenen.

1885 Father dies of a stroke, March 26. Paints *The Potato Eaters*. In November Vincent moves to Antwerp; he is never to return to Holland.

1886 Enrolls at the Royal Academy of Fine Arts, Antwerp, in January, but leaves in haste soon after, possibly not knowing that he had failed his exams and was downgraded in his class; moves to Paris in March to live with his brother Theo. Enters Cormon's studio to study, but stays only a few months. Associates with Emile Bernard, Paul Signac, and Paul Gauguin; influenced by the brighter Impressionist palette. Relationship with Theo becomes strained. Paints over 28 self-portraits while in Paris.

1887 Paints *Lemons, Pears, Apples, Grapes, and an Orange*.

1888 Moves from Paris and arrives in Arles, February 20; lives in Hotel-Restaurant Carrell. Rents the Yellow House in May. Gauguin arrives in October, and paints with Vincent at the Yellow House. On December 23, Vincent mutilates his own ear, and gives it to a local prostitute; the next day he is interned in Arles Hospital after being found close to death; on Christmas day Theo visits.

1889 Returns to studio, January 7. Paints *Self-portrait with Bandaged Ear*. On February 7, Vincent is admitted to hospital for 10 days, then released. In March, some of the citizens of Arles sign a petition to have him sent home or committed to hospital. April 17, Theo marries Johanna Bonger. In May, Vincent decides to enter the asylum at St. Rémy. Paints *Irises* while at the asylum.

1890 January 31, birth of Theo and Jo's son, Vincent. First positive review of Vincent's work, by the critic Albert Aurier. In March, suffers worst ever crisis; readmitted to the asylum. May 16, Vincent leaves St. Rémy, moves to Auvers-sur-Oise; Dr. Gachet, a friend of Camille Pissarro, looks after him. Attempts to commit suicide, July 27, and dies from his injuries, July 29, at the age of 37.

1891 Theo dies, 21 January.

1892 First large retrospective of van Gogh's work organized by the Dutch Symbolist artists, Jan Toorop and Roland Holst.

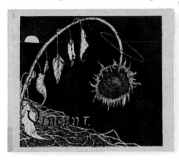

Roland Holst's cover for 1892 van Gogh exhibition catalog

Van Gogh collections around the world

The following shows international museums and galleries that own two or more works by van Gogh. The two main collections of van Gogh are in the Netherlands: paintings and documentation in the Rijksmuseum Vincent van Gogh, Amsterdam; and paintings and drawings in the Rijksmuseum Kröller-Müller, Otterlo.

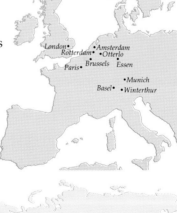

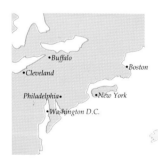

USA
Boston Museum of Fine Arts; Fogg Art Museum (Harvard)
Buffalo The Albright-Knox Art Gallery;
Chicago The Art Institute of Chicago
Cleveland Cleveland Museum of Art
Los Angeles The Armand Hammer Collection
New York Museum of Modern Art; Metropolitan Museum of Art
Philadelphia The Barnes Foundation
Washington D.C. National Gallery of Art

EUROPE
Belgium
Brussels Musée Royaux des Beaux Arts

France
Paris Musée d'Orsay; Musée Rodin

Germany
Essen Folkwang Museum
Munich Bayerische Staatsgemäldsammlungen

Netherlands
Amsterdam Rijksmuseum Vincent van Gogh; Stedelijk Museum
Rotterdam Museum Boysman-van Beuningen
Otterlo Rijksmuseum Kröller-Müller

Russian Federation
St. Petersburg The Hermitage

Switzerland
Basel Offentliche Kunstsammlung
Winterthur Oskar Reinhart Collection

UK
London Courtauld Institute Galleries; National Gallery

ASIA
Japan
Tokyo Bridgestone Museum of Art

Glossary

"Black and White" Artists 19th-century artist/illustrators, who were the first to draw specifically with the intention of having their work printed, particularly engraved.

Brushstrokes The different kind of marks made directly by a brush with oil paint of varying liquidity and thickness; "descriptive" when following the contour of an object or feature, and "directional" when emphasizing the dynamics of a form or composition.

Chiaroscuro (Italian: "light dark") The use of light and shade to model form and create an illusion of depth.

Complementary colors Two colors are "complementary" if they combine to complete the color spectrum. So the complementary of each primary color – red, blue, and yellow – is the combination of the other two. Red and green, blue and orange, and yellow and violet are the basic pairs. In painting, placing complementary colors next to each other makes both appear brighter.

Complementary colors

Engraving A print which is produced by cutting a design into the surface of a wooden or metal plate, then rubbed with ink and printed under heavy pressure.

Etching A method of engraving where a design is cut into a plate with acid, then inked and printed.

Expressionism Use of emphasis or distortion in painting to express an artist's heightened emotions or inner feelings.

Fauve, Fauvism An early 20th-century movement characterized by the use of pure, intense color.

Ground The prepared surface applied to, for example, a canvas, to prevent it reacting with the paint, and to prepare it for painting.

Impasto Paint applied in thick, raised strokes (right).

Impressionists A loose grouping of artists that included Monet, Renoir, Morisot, Pissarro, and Sisley. Their work attempted to capture the ephemeral nature of modern life, using the atmospheric effects of light, and employing various

techniques, including broken color and the emphasis of complementary color.

"Light fast" Until the mid-19th century, pigments were often unstable, and faded in light. Developments in their chemical production meant they became "light fast" – less susceptible to changes in color.

Lithograph A print produced by a method of printing on a metal or stone surface, based on the antipathy of grease and water. A design is drawn in greasy ink or crayon, water applied, and ink remains on the greasy areas, which are then printed, in reverse, on paper.

Modeling Using the brush or pen to indicate solid forms and receding planes on a flat surface.

Pigment The powder color, mineral and aniline, and natural or artificial dyes, used to make paint; when ground together with oil it produces oil paint.

Pre-stretched canvas A canvas that is purchased taut on its stretcher, often pre-prepared with a ground and already primed. Previous to the

Impasto

19th century, artists had commonly stretched and prepared their own canvases.

Priming A stage in the preparation of a canvas where a thin layer of solution is applied on top of ground in order to make it more suitable to receive paint.

Neo-Impressionists The generation of artists who came after the Impressionists, they were associated with using pure, unmixed colors. Included Seurat, Signac, and briefly, Pissarro.

Pointillism A method of painting developed by Georges Seurat, based on optical theory, and involving the applications of paint in separate dots of pure color.

Still life A particular "genre" (or type) of painting showing inanimate objects such as fruit, flowers, or utensils. These are often arranged in a domestic setting.

Symbolism A movement which reacted against Realism, favouring instead a romantic vision of emotions and ideals. Included Puvis de Chavannes, Gustave Moreau, and Odilon Redon.

Van Gogh works on exhibit

The following is a list of the galleries and museums that exhibit the paintings by Vincent van Gogh reproduced in this book.

Unless otherwise stated, all paintings in this book are oil on canvas.

Key: t = top   b = bottom
c = center   l = left   r = right

p. 15 t: *Girl in a Wood*, Rijksmuseum Kröller-Müller, Otterlo, The Netherlands.

p. 16 b: *Farmhouses*, Rijksmuseum Vincent van Gogh, Amsterdam.

p. 17 tr: *Two Peasant Women Digging Potatoes*, Rijksmuseum Kröller-Müller, Otterlo, The Netherlands.

pp. 18–19 c: *Still-life with Birds' Nests*, Rijksmuseum Kröller-Müller, Otterlo, The Netherlands.

p. 20 cl: *Church at Nuenen, with Churchgoers*, Rijksmuseum Vincent van Gogh, Amsterdam.

pp. 20–21 *Open Bible, Extinguished Candle, and Novel*, Rijksmuseum Vincent van Gogh, Amsterdam.

p. 22 *The Potato Eaters*, Rijksmuseum Vincent van Gogh, Amsterdam.

p. 25 bl: *Woman with her Hair Loose*, Rijksmuseum Vincent van Gogh, Amsterdam.

p. 27 *Skull with Burning Cigarette*, Rijksmuseum Vincent van Gogh, Amsterdam.

p. 28 bl: *Plaster Statuette (Type B)*, Rijksmuseum Vincent van Gogh, Amsterdam.

p. 29 tc: *Self-portrait*, 1887, Musée d'Orsay, Paris; br: *The Kingfisher*, Rijksmuseum Vincent van Gogh, Amsterdam.

p. 30 cl: *The Blute Fin*, The Burrell Collection, Glasgow Museums; bl: *Self-portrait with Dark Felt Hat*, Stedelijk Museum, Amsterdam.

pp. 30–31 *The Roofs of Paris*, Rijksmuseum Vincent van Gogh, Amsterdam.

p. 31 tr: *Guingette in Montmartre*, Musée d'Orsay, Paris.

p. 32 br: *Fritillairias*, Musée d'Orsay, Paris.

pp. 34–35 *People in a Park at Asnières*, Rijksmuseum Vincent van Gogh, Amsterdam.

p. 36 tr: *Japonaiserie: The Courtesan (after Keisan Eisen)*, Rijksmuseum Vincent van Gogh, Amsterdam.

p. 37 tr: *Basket with Sprouting Bulbs*, Rijksmuseum Vincent van Gogh, Amsterdam; cr: *Three Novels*, (reverse), Rijksmuseum Vincent

van Gogh, Amsterdam; bl: *Père Tanguy*, Musée Rodin, Paris.

p. 38–39 bl: *Four cut Sunflowers*, Rijksmuseum Kröller-Müller, Otterlo, The Netherlands.

p. 39 tr: *Fourteen Sunflowers*, National Gallery, London.

p. 40 *Lemons, Pears, Apples, Grapes, and an Orange*, Rijksmuseum Vincent van Gogh, Amsterdam.

p. 42 t: *L'Arlésienne*, Musée d'Orsay, Paris; cl: *Eugène Boch*, Musée d'Orsay, Paris; bl: *Café Terrace at Night*, Rijksmuseum Kröller-Müller, Otterlo, The Netherlands.

pp. 42–43 *Night Café*, Yale University Art Gallery, New Haven.

p. 43 br: *Joseph Roulin*, Rijksmuseum Kröller-Müller, Otterlo, The Netherlands.

p. 44 tr: *Peach Trees in Blossom (Souvenir of Mauve)*, Rijksmuseum Kröller-Müller, Otterlo; bl: *Chair with Pipe*, National Gallery, London; br: *The Bedroom*, Musée d'Orsay, Paris.

p. 45 cr: *Memory of the Garden at Etten*, Hermitage Museum, St. Petersburg.

p. 46 *Self-portrait with Bandaged Ear*, Courtauld Institute Galleries, London.

p. 49 cr: *Hospital Saint-Paul*, Musée d'Orsay, Paris; br: *Self-portrait*, 1889, Musée d'Orsay, Paris.

p. 50 b: *Trees with ivy*, Rijksmuseum Vincent van Gogh, Amsterdam.

p. 52 tl: *Peasant Woman Binding Sheaves*, Rijksmuseum Vincent van Gogh, Amsterdam; bl: *Noon: Rest (after Millet)*, Musée d'Orsay, Paris.

p. 53 *Pietà (after Delacroix)*, Rijksmuseum Vincent van Gogh, Amsterdam.

p. 54 *A Cornfield with Cypresses*, National Gallery, London.

p. 56 c: *Branches of an Almond Tree in Blossom*, Rijksmuseum Vincent van Gogh, Amsterdam.

p. 57 tl: *Cypresses with two Figures*, Rijksmuseum Kröller-Müller, Otterlo, The Netherlands.

p. 58 cl: *Dr. Paul Gachet*, Musée d'Orsay, Paris.

p. 59 tl: *Church at Auvers*, Musée d'Orsay, Paris; tr: *Cottages with Thatched Roofs at Cordeville*, Musée d'Orsay, Paris.

pp. 60–61 *Wheatfield with Crows*, Rijksmuseum Vincent van Gogh, Amsterdam.

Index

Acknowledgments

PICTURE CREDITS
Every effort has been made to trace the copyright holders and we apologise in advance for any unintentional omissions. We would be pleased to insert the appropriate acknowledgement in any subsequent edition of this publication.

Key:
t: top *b*: bottom *c*: center *l*: left *r*: right

Abbreviations:
KM: Collection: State Museum Kröller-Müller, Otterlo, The Netherlands
MO: Musée d'Orsay, Paris
NG: Reproduced by courtesy of the Trustees, The National Gallery, London
NO: Nederlands Openlucht Museum, Arnhem
RMN: Réunion des Musées Nationaux
RV: © Roger-Viollet
VGFM: Vincent van Gogh Foundation/Vincent van Gogh Museum, Amsterdam

p1: RMN **p2:** *tl*: Rijksmuseum Vincent van Gogh, Amsterdam; *tr*: VGFM; *cl*: VGFM; *c*: MO; *cr*: VGFM; *bl*: VGFM; *br*: VGFM **p3:** *c*: KM; *cr*: VGFM; *bl*: VGFM; *br*: VGFM **p4:** *tl*: VGFM; *tr*:VGFM; *cl*, *cr*, *bl*, *br*: VGFM **p5:** VGFM **pp6–7:** All images:VGFM **p8:** *t*, *cl*, *bl*, *br*:VGFM **p9:** *t*: VGFM **p10:** *tl*, *cl*, *cr*: VGFM **p11:** *tl*: *God Speed!*, Boughton, Rijksmuseum Vincent van Gogh, Amsterdam; *tr*, *c*: VGFM; *bl*: Bibliothèque Nationale/Jean-Loup Charmet; *br*: KM **p12:** NO; *tr*, *bl*:

VGFM; *br*: MO **p13:** *t*: NO; *b*: VGFM **p14:** *tr*: The Garman Ryan Collection, Walsall Museum and Art Gallery, Walsall, UK; *c*, *bl*: VGFM; *br*: KM **p15:** *t*: KM; *cr*, *cl*: VGFM; *c*, *b*: The Dickens House Museum **p16:** *tr*: VGFM; *cr*: NO; *b*: VGFM **p17:** *tl*: Photo: H. Berssenbrugge Gem. Archief, Tilburg; *tr*: KM; *cl*: KM; *b*: VGFM **p18:** *tr*, *cl*, *b*: VGFM **pp18–19:** *c*: KM **p19:** *tr*: *MO* **p20:** *cl*: VGFM; *c*: *Theodorus van Gogh, Vincent's Father*, Coll. Ellen en Jan Nieuwenhuizen Segaar, The Hague; *b*: Rijksmuseum Vincent van Gogh, Amsterdam **pp20–21:** *c*: VGFM **p21:** *br*: VGFM **p22:** *t*: VGFM **pp22–23:** VGFM **p24:** *tl*, *tr*, *c*, *bl*: VGFM **p25:** *t*: VGFM; Saint Andrieskerk, Antwerp; *bl*: VGFM **p26:** *t*: RV; *cr*: The Trustees of the British Museum; *cr*: VGFM **p27:** *tr*: VGFM; *tr*: Musée Gauguin, Tahiti; *cr*: Toulouse-Lautrec Museum, Albi; *bl*: VGFM, *br*: VGFM **p29:** *tl*: VGFM; *tr*: Ashmolean Museum, Oxford; *cr*: MO; *bl*, *br*: VGFM **p30:** *cl*: Glasgow Museums: The Burrell Collection; *bl*: Stedelijk Museum, Amsterdam **pp30–31:** *c*: VGFM **p31:** *tr*: MO **p32:** *tl*: NG; *tr*, *c*: VGFM; *br*: MO **p33:** *tl*, *c*, *bc*: VGFM; *tr*: NG; *bl*: Courtauld Institute Galleries, London; *br*: RV **p34:** *tl*: Archiv Für Kunst und Geschichte, Berlin; *cl*: *A Sunday on La Grande Jatte*, Seurat, Helen Bartlett Memorial Collection, © 1992 The Art Institute of Chicago, All Rights Reserved; *b*: VGFM **pp34–35:** *c*: VGFM **p35:** *br*: VGFM **p36:** *tr*, *cl*, *bl*, *br*: VGFM **p37:** *tr*, *cr*, *cl*: VGFM; *bl*: *Père Tanguy*, Musée Rodin, Paris/Bridgeman Art Library; *bc*, *br*: VGFM **pp38–39:** *b*: KM **p39:** *tl*: VGFM; *tr*: NG; *br*: VGFM **p40:** VGFM **p42:** *t*: MO; *cr*: MO; *bl*: KM **pp42–43:** *c*: *Night Café*, Yale University Art Gallery, New Haven, Bequest of Stephen Carlton Clark, B.A., 1903 **p43:** *tr*: VGFM; *br*:

KM **p44:** *tl*: VGFM; *tr*: KM; *bl*: NG; *br*: MO **p45:** *t*: *Old Women at Arles*, Gauguin, Helen Birch Bartlett Memorial Collection, photograph © 1992, The Art Institute of Chicago. All Rights Reserved; *tr*, *br*: Musée Gauguin, Tahiti; *cr*: *Memory of the Garden at Etten*, Hermitage Museum, St. Petersburg/Bridgeman Art Library; *bl*: Lefranc & Bourgeois, Le Mans **pp46–47:** Courtauld Institute Galleries, London **p48:** *tl*, *cr*, *b*: VGFM; *cl*: *Arles Hospital*, Collection Oskar Reinhart, Winterthur, Switzerland/Artothek **p49:** *tl*, *tr*, *cl*, *bl*: VGFM; *cr*: MO; *br*: MO **p50:** *c*: VGFM; *b*: VGFM **pp50–51:** *c*: *Irises*, 1888, Collection of the J. Paul Getty Museum, Malibu, California **p51:** *bl*: VGFM **p52:** *tl*: VGFM; *cl*, *cr*: VGFM; *bl*: MO **p53:** *t*: VGFM; *bl*, *br*: VGFM **pp54–55:** NG **p56:** *tl*, *cr*, *cl*: VGFM; *tr*: Photo Reindert Groot, courtesy of Rijksmuseum Vincent van Gogh, Amsterdam; *bl*: Tate Gallery, London; *br*: RMN **p58:** *tl*: VGFM; *tr*: RMN; *cl*: MO; *cr*: KM **p59:** *tl* MO; *tr*: MO; *cr*, *b*: VGFM **p60:** *t*: VGFM **pp60–61:** *c*: VGFM **p61:** *tl*, *tr*: VGFM **p62:** *c*: VGFM **p63** *c*:VGFM **p64:** *tr*: *A Cornfield With Cypresses* (detail), NG; *bl*: *Fritillairias* (detail), MO **Front cover:** Clockwise from top left: VGFM; VGFM; MO; VGFM; VGFM; VGFM; NG; VGFM **Back cover**: VGFM; VGFM; VGFM; VGFM; NG; *A Cornfield with Cypresses* (detail), NG (also *c*, *cr*); VGFM; VGFM; VGFM; RMN **Inside front flap:** *t*: VGFM; *b*: MO

Additional Photography:
Steve Gorton: **p3:** *cl*; **p19:** *cr*; **p26:** *b*; **p50:** *tl*; Philippe Sebert: **p12:** *br*; **p29:** *cr*; **p31:** *tr*; **p42:** *br*; **p44:** *t*; **p49:** *cr*, *br*; **p54:** *t*; **p58:** *bl*; **p59:** *tl*, *tr*; Peter Chadwick: **p16:** *bl*; Philip Gatward: **p28:** *tr*; **p39:** *tl*; **p43:** *br*; Dave King: **p40:** *tl*, *tr*; Colin Keates: **p50:** *tc*; **p51:** *br*; Andreas Einsiedel: **p52:** *b*;

Andrew McRobb: **p58:** *b*.
Additional picture research: Caroline Lucas

Dorling Kindersley would like to thank:
Mrs. Daalder-Vos and Mrs. Feuth of the Stedelijk Museum, Amsterdam, for their endless patience and cooperation; Mrs. Pabst of the Rijksmuseum Vincent van Gogh, Amsterdam, for her enthusiastic research assistance; Mr. Robert Bruce-Gardner, Director of Conservation and Technology, Courtauld Institute of Art, London, for his advice on technical analysis; the staff at the National Gallery, London; Caroline Juler for editorial assistance; Julia Harris-Voss for picture credits; Hilary Bird for the index. Maps: James Mills-Hicks

Author's acknowledgments:
No book on Vincent van Gogh can be compiled or written without reference to Jan Hulsker's "The Complete Van Gogh," and more recently his "Vincent and Theo van Gogh – a dual Biography." Other sources of reference include Ronald Pickvance's "Van Gogh in Arles" and "Van Gogh in St. Rémy and Auvers;" "Van Gogh – a Retrospective," edited by Susan Alyson Stein; "Young Vincent" by Martin Bailey; and "The Seven Sketchbooks of Vincent van Gogh" by Johannes van der Wolk. I would also like to thank Richard Kendall and Ken Wilkie for their advice. At Dorling Kindersley, I have been extremely grateful for the patience and kindness of Mark Johnson Davies, Phil Hunt, Luisa Caruso, and Sean Moore.

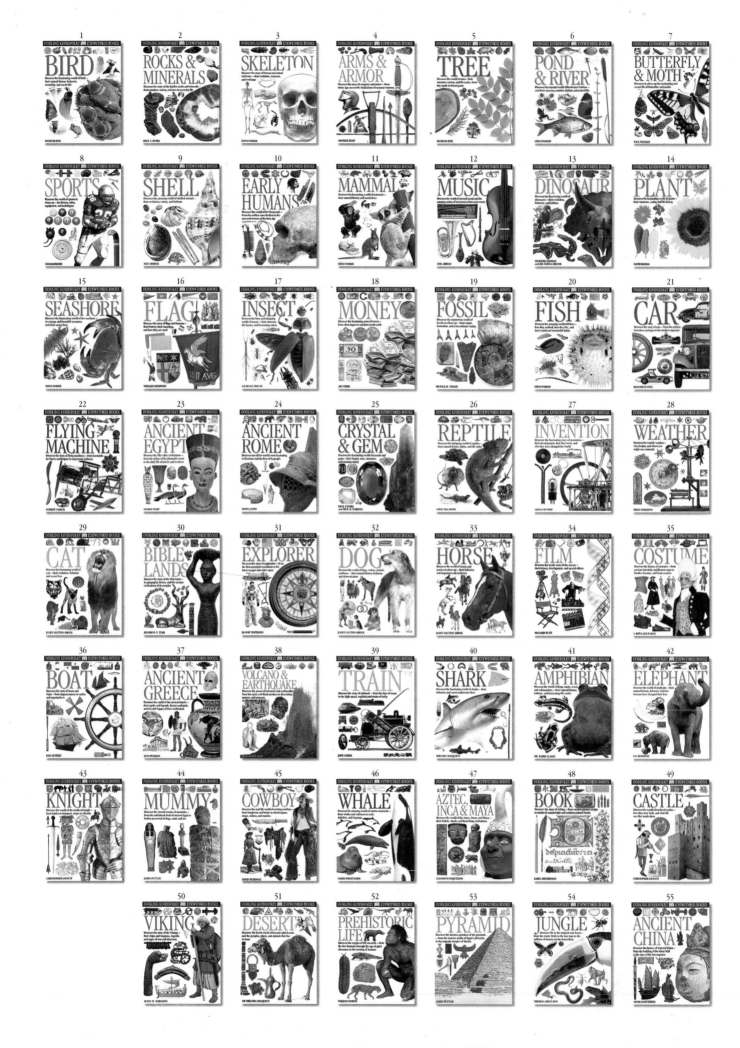